Boomer Consumer

Ten New Rules for Marketing to America's Largest, Wealthiest and Most Influential Group

By Matt Thornhill and John Martin

A LINX Book

Books are available for special promotions and premiums. For details contact Special Markets, LINX, Corp., Box 613, Great Falls, VA 22066 or email specialmarkets@linxcorp.com

Printed in the United States of America.

Book Design by Paul Fitzgerald
Editing by Sandra Gurvis

ISBN 0-9642386-7-5

www.boomerconsumer.com

*To the most generous and loving
person in the world, my mother, Jane,
who dedicated her life to four of
the 78 million Boomers.*

- John Martin

*To the love of my life, Ellen,
who inspires me every day while
raising the next generation.*

- Matt Thornhill

Acknowledgments

This book is like many business books in that it took a village to make it happen. We would like to thank our many villagers.

The Elders – those who understood the age wave and the new consumer majority of older Boomers, Dr. Ken Dychtwald and David Wolfe. Thanks also to Brent Green, Vicki Thomas, Chuck Nyren, Mary Furlong, Richard Adler, Dr. Neal Cutler and all those other business, academic and scientific minds that have explored an aging population long before we came on the scene.

The Scouts – those who helped us find our way in the early days, like Pete Boisseau, Wilson Flohr, Deborah Usry, Robin Raff and Bob Rayner, who first wrote our story in the media.

The Merchants – those who first gave us a platform for sharing our work, including Bill Baxter and Jenny Price of Retail Merchants Association, Rob Methven of Genworth Financial, Tom Silvestri of Media General, and Jessica Velazquez of Centro de Soluciones in the country of Panama. Plus, of course, our many clients over the last four years that have enabled us to spread our wings and fly.

The Locals – those who joined forces with us, like Art Webb and Mary Pannullo of BCF, Sharon Lilly, Chris Bonney, Walt Tudor, Jocelyn Tice, Rachel Burgess, Sandra Baker, John Judy, David Darnell, Laura Turner Reid, Bethany Taylor, and Dr. Karen Smith.

The Spectators – those thousands and thousands of subscribers and audience members that have encouraged us to keep spreading the gospel of today's Boomer Consumer.

The Experts – those professionals who made this book a reality, publisher Steve Eunpu, editor extraordinaire, Sandra Gurvis, and designer Paul Fitzgerald.

The Families – for Matt: wife Ellen, children Allison, Clark, Sam and Mia. For John: wife Sara, children Coldon, Derek and Rebecca.

The Partner – last but not least, we thank our Generation X business partner, Elizabeth McLaughlin. She demonstrated great patience, allowing two Boomers to take time away from running a company to write this book about Boomers. We thank you.

Table *of* Contents

78 million Baby Boomers, born between 1946-64, dominate American politics, business, entertainment and culture. Here is a listing of over 1,000 of the most influential: ....▶

Introduction

Four years ago, we came across the astounding statistic that every seven seconds, a Baby Boomer was turning 50 years old somewhere in America. This meant that approximately 10,000 Boomers turn 50 every day, 365 days a year.

After spending over two decades in the advertising business, focusing our clients' money and attention on young adults ages 18-49, we realized this was a seismic shift, a veritable demographic earthquake. Since Boomers were departing the "coveted" 18-49 segment in droves, marketers were perhaps now ignoring them. For the last 40 years, marketing had been focused almost exclusively on the 18-49 year old group. If you were over 50, marketers either pretended you were dead or lumped you into a group called "seniors."

If they were anything like us or our Boomer colleagues and friends, it was a pretty safe bet that Boomer Consumers were neither dead nor "seniors." While it was true that Boomers over 50 were no longer young adults, they hardly seemed willing to accept the "senior" label anytime soon. Boomer Consumers over 50 are a new demographic segment, with vast reserves of disposable income and anxious to spend it on new products and services. And many marketers had no idea how to relate to this audience.

We saw the passage of Boomers through the mid-century mark as an opportunity to help marketers everywhere. We analyzed, researched and studied the demographic to learn how Boomers today, especially those over 50, think, feel and respond to selling, advertising and marketing messages. The Boomer Project was formed and quickly joined forces with SIR Research, a national consumer marketing research firm in Richmond, Virginia with 43 years of experience, and with Survey Sampling International, a Fairfield, Connecticut-based firm specializing in providing survey participants from around the U.S.

Our first research study in late 2003 was small, with 400 participants, but it proved that Boomers over 50 already felt ignored by marketers and advertising. In fact, some 66% expressed the opinion that marketers were targeting either someone younger or older. These Boomer Consumers felt like they were being overlooked.

Vladimir Putin :: Condoleezza Rice :: :: :: **Boomer Governors:** Sarah Palin/Alaska :: Janet Napolitano/

Four years and several national studies later, the Boomer Project continues to work towards understanding the current mindset of today's older Boomer Consumer in terms of selling, advertising and marketing messages. We now travel the country speaking at conferences, trade shows, company events and training sessions. We work with companies and organizations of all shapes and sizes to educate and enlighten sales, marketing and customer service personnel about today's older Boomer Consumer. We do product development projects and we track the latest and most important trends in Boomer marketing and report on it in a monthly newsletter, *Boomer Marketing News*. Details on subscribing to the newsletter, along with additional information and resources are available on our Web site, www.boomerproject.com.

The purpose of this book is to spread the word on Boomer Consumers to smart marketers and business people everywhere. To that end, it is organized into two main sections: **Understanding the Boomer Consumer Today** and the **New Rules for Selling & Marketing to Today's Boomer Consumer.** The first section provides an overview on Boomers – who and where they are, what they buy and the Boomer culture in general. We'll explore this and apply it to selling and marketing to Boomers today.

It delves into three areas of study: Psychology, Sociology and Anthropology. The chapter on Boomer Psychology is designed to help you understand where Boomers are now in their cognitive and psychological development. Knowing what's going on in their heads and in their lives, including the underlying motivations behind their behavior, is the first step in determining how to more effectively reach them with sales and marketing messages.

The chapter on Boomer Sociology will provide insight into the various life stages and lifestyles of Boomer Consumer today. Obviously Boomers have a completely different way of doing things from previous generations. Understanding the why and how of these differences will help you connect with Boomers more than, for example, knowing how old they are.

The Anthropology chapter offers a closer look at the shared culture and history of Boomers and the events that shaped their generation.

Arizona :: Mike Beebe/Arkansas :: Arnold Schwarzenegger/California :: Bill Ritter/Colorado :: Jodi Rell/Con-

Ultimately, what binds one generation and makes it different from another is its place in time and history. The experiences shared by 78 million American Baby Boomers during their "Wonder Bread Years" of the 1950s, '60s and '70s have had a tremendous impact on who they are and how they think. We'll explore this and apply it to marketing and selling to Boomer Consumers today.

The second section of the book, the **New Rules for Selling & Marketing to Today's Boomer Consumer**, consists of ten "rules" uncovered in our work with and research of this demographic. Rather than being hard and fast, they are more of a checklist, designed to help you better design sales, marketing and advertising materials to appeal to the over-50 Boomer Consumer. These rules include things like why it is important to use emotionally-compelling concepts, words and images in your marketing efforts, and why your message has to be couched in the positive, not the negative, in order to get the attention of today's Boomer. Along with offering insight, they will give you practical tools and techniques that can be put to immediate use when marketing to Boomers.

The book concludes with a look at what we've come to define as the **"Golden" Rule** of selling, marketing and advertising to today's Boomer Consumer. It's our prediction of the underlying motivation and driver for all Boomer behavior in the next 20-40 years. We won't give it away here, but feel free to jump ahead to take a peek.

Each chapter begins with a short story or anecdote about a typical Baby Boomer, someone born between 1946 and 1964. These are real people we know, but we have changed the names and modified a few details to keep their identities private.

We've also created a companion Web site, www.boomerconsumer.com, which has more information and tools to help reinforce many of the concepts we discuss. The site can be accessed by the user name "boomer" and the password "c0nsum3r" using the number "0" and "3" where underlined.

necticut :: Charlie Crist/Florida :: Sonny Perdue/Georgia :: Linda Lingle/Hawaii :: Rod Blagojevich/Illinois ::

Although this book provides a basic primer and starting point, Boomers, being what they are, will remain a moving target. More will reach 50, 60, and then 70 with each passing year. How they react to sales, marketing and advertising messages today will change as they grow older and, dare we say, mature.

Rest assured that we'll stay on the case and in the marketplace talking to Boomer Consumers. We will report what we learn, online and with updates to this book.

Welcome to the dawn of the Middle Age of Aquarius. What a long, strange trip it will continue to be.

O'Malley/Maryland :: Deval Patrick/Massachusetts :: Jennifer Granholm/Michigan :: Tim Pawlenty/Minnesota

Part 1
Understanding the
Boomer Consumer Today

Part 1 Introduction:

The Baby Boomer generation is America's largest, wealthiest and most influential, one that marketers today cannot afford to ignore. We will share the numbers behind this generation, and their self image about their seemingly never-ending "Middle Age."

Our approach to look at Boomer Psychology, Sociology and Anthropology, or culture, provides the appropriate lens to see today's Boomer Consumers, is based in part on what demographers call the "age/period/cohort" problem. Demographers and academics who study generations will tell you it is impossible to separate the three aspects when determining how a generation might behave.

"Age" refers to the physical and psychological age of the subject. "Period" refers to the specific time and events in history. "Cohort" is the generational grouping to which the subject belongs. Here's an example of the dilemma: September 11, 2001. How an individual responded to that event is based on how old they were at the time – their age. A 71-year-old responded to it differently than a 51-year-old and a 31-year-old and an 11-year-old. "Age" is the first factor to consider. The event also happened during a time in history when terrorists were striking virtually everywhere but in America, so the time "period" in history when this event occurred is unique and important. Lastly, each generational "cohort" responded differently. Those GI and Silent Generation members may have recalled their feelings on December 7, 1941. Boomers may have thought about their feelings when JFK or Martin Luther King, Jr. were killed. Generation X may have been thinking about the Challenger disaster, or Columbine. Each generation processes the event differently.

The problem with separating age from period from cohort cannot be solved. For marketers trying to understand today's Boomer Consumer, the focus should be on understanding their current age, about 40 to 60 years old, their current life stages and life styles, and their generational traits that bind them together into one cohort.

We'll start there. Then we'll move on to how marketers at companies and organizations can better construct messages to better connect with these Boomers.

Hampshire :: Jon Corzine/New Jersey :: Bill Richardson/New Mexico :: Eliot Spitzer/New York :: Mike Easley/

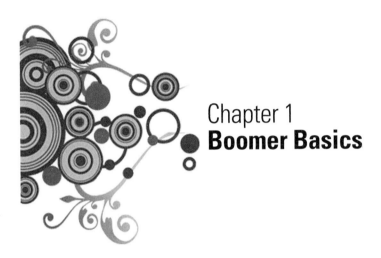

Chapter 1
Boomer Basics

North Carolina :: John Hoeven/North Dakota :: Brad Henry/Oklahoma :: Mark Sanford/South Carolina :: Mike

Wilson Wald entered college in 1968 as a conservative, quiet boy from Worthington, Ohio, and graduated four years later as a pot-smoking, long-haired, and married hippie. Neither the hair nor the marriage lasted, and Wilson ventured off to New York City. His first job was in a small advertising agency, before he joined on with an entertainment venture called the Walt Disney Company.

From New York to Orlando to North Carolina and ultimately back to Florida, Wilson pursued a career in theme park management. He remarried long ago and he prefers "Gramps" over any other moniker these days.

Wilson is very busy in his community, serving on several boards for non-profits. He runs three days a week and loves green tea. Wilson may be on the high end of the income range for most Boomers, but he is most certainly a Boomer Consumer.

He owns two iPods, recently traded in a Mercedes for a Range Rover, bought a new Samsung HDTV and is always looking to add to his collection of Hermes ties. He has a second home at a ski resort and takes mini-vacations with his wife about once every two months.

Despite his "conspicuous consumption," to most marketers, Wilson has not existed since the year 2000, when he turned 50 years old. To them, he might as well be dead.

Rounds/South Dakota :: Rick Perry/Texas :: Jon Huntsman/Utah :: Jim Douglas/Vermont :: Tim Kaine/Virginia ::

Introduction: Meet the Boomers

During the 18 years after the GIs came home from Europe from World War II, from 1946 through 1964, live births in America jumped from less than 2 million a year to 3.5-4.2 million a year. The term that described this generation — "Baby Boomer" — came into popular use in 1980 with the publication of *Great Expectations: America and the Baby Boom Generation* by Landon Y. Jones.

Baby Boomers were the first to be raised in front of the TV, during the Cold War and Vietnam. They remember the deaths of JFK, RFK and MLK Jr. Images and memories of protests against the war and for Civil Rights, Watergate, *M*A*S*H, All in the Family* and Elvis have been burned upon their collective consciousness.

Boomers have been driving the engine of the American economy since they came of age in the 1970s. Since they made up the bulk of the 18-49 year old demographic group, they have been the focus of practically everything, including virtually all marketing and advertising as well as books, movies, and TV shows. It truly was "all about them."

The year 1996, however, marked a dramatic change in the landscape for those trying to sell, market and advertise to Boomers: They began to turn 50 years old. And not just a few; in great masses, as they've done through the decades because there are so many of them. (You may have noticed that Boomers rarely do anything halfway.)

Since 1996, over half of the cohort has reached the mid-century point. By January 1, 2015, all of the Boomers will have traveled around the sun some 50 or more times.

That means most Boomers are no longer "young adults," part of the 18-49 segment. Nor are they part of the traditional over-50 set, or "seniors." In fact, Boomers like Wilson Wald are a new, separate demographic segment, at new, different stages of life. Selling and marketing to them will require the new set of guidelines described and discussed in this book.

Chris Gregoire/Washington :: Joe Manchin/West Virginia :: Dave Freudenthal/Wyoming   ::   ::   :: **Boomer**

Our goal is to help you understand today's Boomer Consumer – where they are in life's journey; how they think, feel and respond to selling, marketing and advertising messages; and how to more effectively connect with them. We will spend one paragraph on <u>why</u> you should target Boomers, and then the rest of the book will focus on <u>how</u> to do it.

First, let's get oriented to the overall numbers for the five current generations alive today in the United States, based on live births during the relevant years:

GI Generation	1905-25	50,000,000
Silent Generation	1926-45	35,000,000
Baby Boomers	1946-64	78,000,000
Generation X	1965-82	65,000,000
Millennials	1983-02?	80,000,000

Source: U.S. Census 2006

The Boomer generation is almost as large as the previous two generations combined, and is 11% bigger than Generation X segment that follows it. The Millennials (also known as Generation Y), are as large as the Boomers, but there is no agreement as to when that generation ends and the next, as yet-unnamed one begins. Most demographers say it takes about ten years after the end of cohort before they can determine the logical end date or generational divide of that cohort.

BoomBox

Well, Duh: It's the Demography, Part 1

In his book, *Common Census,* Ken Gronbach presents a strong argument for marketers to wake up and read the Census data. As the 78 million member Boomer generation ages out of child-rearing years and into their empty nesting years, countless industries and categories will be transformed.

CEOs: Richard Adkerson/Freeport Copper :: Anthony Alexander/FirstEnergy :: John Allison/BB&T ::

Look at the shrinking sales of GAP and other 20-something clothing stores. Is it bad marketing or simply the fact that there are 19% fewer Gen Xers than there were Boomers?

On the other end of the age spectrum, Gronbach points out that the last of the GI Generation will be departing from Assisted Living facilities in the coming years, and there are millions fewer Silent Generation members to take their place. Boomers are 20+ years away from needing Assisted Living facilities.

As Gronbach so aptly puts it, when the Assisted Living industry complains over next 20 years "Where did all the seniors go?" — the answer is, **"They were never born!"**

Why Market to Boomers?

We promised one paragraph as to why marketers should still be focusing on today's Boomer Consumer. Here it is: According to the 2006 Bureau of Labor Statistics Consumer Expenditure Study, the 78 million Boomers are at their peak earning years and spend more money annually on consumer goods and services on a per capita basis than any other generation. Plus, there are so many more Boomers than other generations that when you multiply the per capita figure by 78 million you realize that today's Boomer Consumer spends some $2.3 trillion annually on consumer goods and services. *That's some $400 billion more than any other cohort!*

There are dozens of other economic reasons to focus on Boomers, but we think $400 billion is significant enough to at least get the attention of CEOs and CFOs in most companies, if not the marketing department.

With $400 billion as our starting point on this journey, our next stop is not todays Boomer Consumer, but you. To get the most benefit out of this book, consider one important but simple premise: *Consumers over the age of 50 will buy things marketed to them.* Why, of course, you say, that's easy to agree with. Yet for the last 40 years, most marketers have acted like that isn't true. Marketers have focused exclusively on consumers 18-49. They have long believed that consumers over 50 are too set in their ways and pre-determined in their brand choices that no amount of effort will dislodge them into considering another product or service.

Here's the truth, especially as it relates to Boomer Consumers over 50: *They aren't about to stop consuming just because they've reached life's midpoint. If anything, they are only halfway done.*

For example, according to studies from the automobile industry, the typical American will buy and own 13 cars in their lifetime. Seven of those cars are likely to be purchased *after* the age of 50. We can tell you right now those Boomer Consumers over 50 won't be buying their father's Oldsmobile. Okay, GM stopped making Oldsmobile, but the point is that they will likely be buying luxury or high-end cars. Yet few car manufacturers are targeting older Boomers with their luxury models. They are missing the boat – or shall we say the automobile – in a big way.

Your Mind-Set Matters

By now you're starting to realize that there is some strange thinking taking place out there in marketing land if we have to begin this book by practically begging you to acknowledge the fact that Boomer Consumers over 50 have money to spend and interest in spending it on goods and services. If you're like us, you see the irony in the popular marketing assumption that when consumers turn 50, they become so set in their ways they won't try new brands. The irony is that the only people "set in their ways" are the marketers themselves, clinging to what is clearly a myth in marketing, established when Boomer Consumers themselves were 49 and younger.

The research firm RoperASW was hired a few years ago by AARP to learn more about brand loyalty among consumers of different ages and whether consumers make brand choices early in life and stick with them. The study found that these days, few, if any, consumers at any age are particularly brand loyal. Overall, most (91%) of consumers agree that they care mostly about "value" and not "brand name." Moreover, when deciding on a particular brand, the most important thing is "that it gives good value for the money" said 66% of all Americans, no matter what their age.

The RoperASW study concluded that in only a few categories do consumers make brand choices early in life and stay with them. Items such as toothpaste, bath soap, or laundry detergent tend to be decided upon at a young age and rarely changed; that is, until the marketers themselves make product enhancements, alterations and improvements, which can diffuse loyalty across many flavors, forms, and other permutations. Today is someone a loyal Crest toothpaste consumer or are they loyal to toothpastes with whiteners and baking soda, no matter the brand name? How about laundry detergent: Is it Tide that matters most now or "No additives or perfumes?" Even loyalty to brands in previously "set" categories can be a fleeting thing.

The RoperASW study also found that younger consumers in their 20's and 30's are in fact *more* brand loyal that Boomers. Actually, this doesn't surprise us, and you'll learn why in Chapter 2 when we explore more about Boomer Psychology.

Now that we've shown what a rich marketing segment Boomers over 50 can be, here's another concept: Boomers at age 50, some of whom began turning age 60 in 2006, are not "old." They don't think of themselves as "old" and will ignore any sales or marketing message targeting "the old." "Old Age" is something Boomers see far off into the future - if at all - perhaps happening by the time they reach their mid-70s. Maybe.

Today's Boomer Consumer is, on average, 51 years old. That means "Old Age" won't happen until 24 or so years into the future (2030 for that median-aged Boomer). Although Boomer Consumers can and do admit that they are in "Middle Age" and may even confess, grudgingly, that they are "growing older," they aren't "old" yet.

Babb/Comerica :: Douglas Baker/Ecolab :: Steve Ballmer/Microsoft :: Brenda Barnes/Sara Lee :: John Barth/

In our national study of Boomer Consumers and younger adults, we asked the question "At what age is someone over the hill?" Boomer Consumers said someone is over the hill at age 75. Some Boomers answered: "Never." "Over the hill isn't an age, it's an attitude." "It's up to the individual." "I'll be over the hill when I'm six feet under the hill." "When they close the box."

But that isn't what we heard from young adults, those Gen Xer's and Millennials in our study. Our research showed that those young adults, perhaps even the very one responsible for selling, marketing and advertising to these Boomers, see someone as "over the hill" at age 57! You can see how this could cause conflict between Boomers and young adults about marketing today. Boomers see themselves still years away from being "over the hill" while young adults think leading edge Boomers are already on the down slope.

When we share this finding at conferences and speaking events, the Boomers in the audience always gasp and groan, realizing how misguided young adults are as to where "the hill" is. Perhaps we've identified one of the major reasons why Boomer Consumers tell us they believe marketing and advertising is targeting either older or younger people. No one seems to be focusing and connecting with Boomer Consumers today. To paraphrase the song, the times they need a' changing.

"Nature" vs. "Nurture" for the Boomer Consumer Generation

Understanding human behavior has been simplified into "Nature" and "Nurture." "Nature" means our behavior comes from within, perhaps hardwired into our DNA at the instant of conception; and therefore, we act the way we do simply because of the way we were born. "Nurture" asserts that our behavior is learned and therefore can be modified.

We have uncovered two camps with regard to Baby Boomers and generational differences. One group attributes Boomer Consumer behavior to underlying human motivations and cognitive development, or "Nature." The other believes Boomer Consumer behavior comes from "Nurture" or what we call "generational zeitgeist."

Johnson Controls :: Paul Beideman/Associated Banc-Corp :: Stephen Bennett/Intuit :: Daniel Berce/AmeriCredit

Zeitgiest is a German expression that means "the spirit *(Geist)* of the time *(Zeit)*." It denotes the intellectual and cultural climate of an era and the ethos of a cohort of people that spans one or more subsequent generations. Despite their diverse age and socio-economic background, they experience a certain worldview, which is prevalent at a particular time period. It is "zeitgeist" that unites 78 million Boomers over an 18-year span into a single cohort.

Our research on today's Boomer Consumers tells us that their behavior is a combination of "Nature" and "Nurture." A grasp of basic human psychological and physiological development will certainly help us better understand Boomer behavior today. But viewing this behavior through the lens of generational zeitgeist will help us truly get a handle on what makes a Boomer tick.

For example, during their youth and especially their late teens and early twenties, Boomers drove the liberal, free-spirited "anti-establishment" movement of the late 1960s and 1970s. "Don't trust anyone over 30" was the popular refrain. Some would say it's ironic that those same Boomer Consumers, now in their 50's, are the "Establishment."

It may in fact be ironic, but it is also natural. In most societies, adults 40 to 60 years old run things. By simply reaching that age, Boomers became the "Establishment."

Nevertheless, things are different today than when Boomers were in their early twenties. For example:

- The role of women in society has changed. Women work in many different types of careers and are active in sports and the military.

- Minorities are more accepted - and in fact much of their culture is part of the popular mainstream, especially among younger people. They have educational and job opportunities that had previously been unavailable to them.

:: William Berkley/WR Berkley :: Jeff Bezos/Amazon.com :: Bryce Blair/Avalonbay Communities :: Alan Boeck-

- Consumers are more environmentally aware, expressing concerns over oil usage and the "greenhouse effect."

- Homosexuality is more in the mainstream of society, rather than being hidden "in the closet."

These and many other changes may not have been initiated by Boomers, but many Boomers pushed for them, working to make them permanent, due in part to their generational zeitgeist, or place in time.

We'll explore the nature aspect of today's Boomer Consumer in the next chapter and the nurture component in Chapter 4. Both are important in understanding today's Boomer Consumer.

Understanding the Numbers

Some 78 million Boomers were born between 1946-64. According to author Landon Jones, the first Boomer was Kathleen Casey-Kirschling of Philadelphia. Kathy was born one second after midnight on January 1, 1946. As the first Boomer, Kathy gets her "15 minutes of fame" every ten years or so, when the media interviews her for stories about the first Boomers turning 40, 50, and now 60.

But what about the other 77,999,999 Boomers? Here are some facts:

- Every day, 10,000 more of them turn 50 years old.

- One out of every three adults over 21 in the country is a Baby Boomer.

- 88% have married, 41% of those have since divorced. Some 12% never married, double the percentage of previous generations.

- 83% have children, but 34% are now empty nesters.

- 37% of the Boomer parents are also grandparents. Half of all grandparents alive today are Boomers.

mann/Fluor :: Jon Boscia/Lincoln National :: Jack Bovender/HCA :: Gregory Boyce/Peabody Energy :: George

- Only 24% say they've experienced a "mid-life crisis."

- Already, 30% say they've survived a major illness, and 32% have changed their diet due to a medical condition.

- 93% of Boomers state that exercise is a primary way to manage healthy aging. Only 27% do it regularly, and only 21% do it infrequently. That means 53% don't bother at all.

Source: Natural Marketing Institute "Boomers and Healthy Aging" study, 2005

As we said earlier, Boomers also don't see themselves as old...yet. They still consider themselves middle-aged. One might argue that today's Boomer Consumers are fooling themselves, that 60 is indeed old. But in truth, as gerontologist Ken Dychtwald often says, Boomers are the first generation in the history of the world to reach this milestone and to know, with reasonable certainty, that they will probably live another 30-40 years. Our parents thought they'd live to about age 75, which is why retiring at 65 made sense.

Boomers, on the other hand, see themselves living to age 90 and beyond. Given that, it comes as no surprise that they tell us in survey after survey that they won't reach "Old Age" until they are almost 80. Boomers have extended "Middle Age" to practically last a lifetime.

Recent proof of this remarkable stretching can be found in a cover story in the October 2005 *BusinessWeek*. The feature was about "aging Boomers," who at the time were 41-59 years old. Not "old," but simply "aging." It was a terrific piece and offered good tips on how to best connect with what the editors called "Middle Aged Boomers."

Shortly after it appeared, Vicki Thomas, who for 20 years has run a Connecticut-based marketing consultancy focused on marketing to older Americans, had the nagging feeling that she had seen this story before in *BusinessWeek*. She rummaged through the files in her basement and found a cover story on "Those aging Baby Boomers" from May 1991 (when Boomers were 27-45 years old).

Vicki's find astonished us. Baby Boomers had pulled off one of the greatest tricks in history – they had stopped time for 14 years! How else could we get from 1991 to 2005 and still have a prevailing perception that Boomers are "aging." It seems they haven't actually "aged" at all!

This phenomenon is perhaps the Boomer generation's greatest contribution to American society. They have made it okay to be a "mature" adult for a long, long time – approximately from your early 30's through your late 70's. Before that you're in your "Youth" and after than you're in "Old Age." In-between, for upwards of 40 years, you're Middle Aged.

Another aspect of today's Boomer Consumer and their mindset about growing older is that they feel much younger than they are. In our research, we ask consumers to tell how old they "feel," as a way to gauge their psychological age. In the studies, younger adults, those with an average age of 30, typically feel their age. But older respondents tell us they feel years younger than they are. Boomers, in fact, tell us they feel at least ten years younger than their actual age, and Boomers over 50 feel 14 years younger. That means that a typical 54-year-old Boomer feels about 40.

This finding appears to reassure marketers who have continually been targeting the "golden" demographic of 18-49. They tell us, "See, we don't need to target Boomers over 50 because they still feel 40 years old. We reach them with marketing that targets the 18-49 segment."

However, it doesn't work that way. While a Boomer over 50 may still *feel* as if they are 40 years old, they are not the same person as when they were 40. They've changed — grown, developed, and matured. They are in fact, different people than when they were 40. Are you the same person today you were 10 years ago?

We'll learn more about these changes in Chapter 2. How old someone "feels" is only one aspect to understanding where they are in life, and how to market to them.

Kevin Burke/Consolidated Edison :: Michael Burns/Dana :: John Cahill/Pepsi Bottling Group :: Louis Camilleri/

Well, Duh: It's the Demography, Part 2

Reading *Common Census* made us go back and pour over U.S. Census data ourselves. According to the Census, between now and 2017, the U.S. adults 18+ population will increase by 23.5 million people, with immigration, deaths and those under 18 aging into the segment. But interestingly, here's how it breaks down: 22.5 million of that increase will happen in the 50+ segment. Only one million new 18-49 adults are anticipated.

That's right, that "golden" demographic of 18-49 will be a stagnant wasteland for the next ten years while the 50+ segment will jump 23%.

The reason is simple: it's those Baby Boomers reaching age 50 and beyond. They are moving out of 18-49 and will essentially be replaced by Millennials reaching age 18 and older. By 2015 all Boomers will be over 50 (in fact, the last Boomer hits 50 on December 31, 2014). Even those who don't put much stock in the future – or in change - can see the numbers and realize it's time to shift focus from marketing to 18-49 exclusively and include the 50+ segment.

The facts – and figures – add up.

In 2003, a Harris poll was conducted on the "ideal age" for Americans. "Ideal age" was defined as the age at which one would want to stay forever. Up until age 35 or so, most folks responded that the ideal age was in front of them. Older respondents, those over age 35, said the "ideal age" had already passed.

Altria Group :: Lewis Campbell/Textron :: Mitchell Caplan/E-Trade Financial :: Chase Carey/Directv Group ::

Harris Interactive Poll # 61, October 22, 2003
The Ideal Age, if you could live forever at that age:

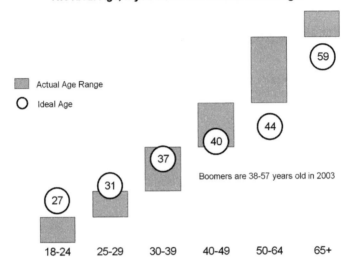

Actual Age Range

○ Ideal Age

Boomers are 38-57 years old in 2003

| 18-24 | 25-29 | 30-39 | 40-49 | 50-64 | 65+ |

Source: Harris Interactive

Boomers, of course, view the ideal age as significantly younger than they are today. Older generations, those over age 65, also think the ideal age is younger, but not quite to the same extent as the youth-oriented Boomers. It doesn't matter whether you are in the Boomer, Silent or GI generation, if you're over 35, you typically think the ideal age is younger than your actual age. It's natural.

Perhaps you are now seeing the need for this book: Younger people think 57 is "over the hill," while Boomers at age 57 feel like they are in their mid-40's, with "Old Age" still 20+ years in the future. Many involved in the marketing and advertising industry are themselves under 40, so we're not surprised when today's Boomer Consumer told us in our first national study in 2003 that they feel marketing and advertising is targeting either someone older (66%) or younger (62%). Boomers believe marketers simply don't understand them these days.

And who can blame them? An evening of prime-time television often consists of youth-oriented commercials for beer or auto insurance or demeaning spots for incontinence or denture adhesive. Throw in the usual glut of pharmaceutical ads for every conceivable ailment and condition

Richard Carrion/Popular :: Gregory Case/Aon :: Clarence Cazalot/Marathon Oil :: John Chambers/Cisco Systems

and it is enough to make you "mute" the commercials or get a DVR so you can fast-forward through them.

Let's work together to create a new understanding of marketing to today's Boomer consumer. Don't we owe that to Wilson Wald and all the other Middle-Aged Aquarians?

BoomBox

Boomer Consumers, Global Trends and the Longevity Revolution

- The 20th century is known as the "Century of Population Growth." The 21st will be the "Century of Population Aging."

- By 2050, the median age worldwide will be 38, up from 28 in 2000 and 24 in 1950.

- In the US, the median age will be 41 in 2050. In Italy, it will be 53!

- The Baby Boom occurred in practically all developed countries after WWII, so the U.S. is not alone in battling this population bulge.

- Overall, Europe's population has stopped growing and is now shrinking.

- By 2050, the four largest countries by population will be India, China, United States and Pakistan.

- US population growth is driven by immigration; our fertility rate is at the rate of sustaining the population, not growing it.

- In 2000 there were 250,000 people worldwide over 100. By 2050, there will be 3.8 million.

Source: *United Nations Population Division*

:: John Chapple/Nextel :: Ken Chenault/American Express :: Michael Cherkasky/Marsh & McLennan :: Bruce

Summary

This chapter introduced you to today's Boomer Consumer, with a snapshot of who and where they are. It also provided fair warning:

- Boomers at 50 and older aren't anywhere near done consuming. They will buy things marketed to them for 20 or more years.

- Boomers aren't particularly brand loyal or set in their ways, opening the door for talented marketers to persuade them to try new products and services.

- In their minds, Boomers over 50 aren't "old" or even close to "over the hill." They are in what they themselves call "Middle Age," which can stretch almost 50 years, until they reach about 80. Boomers will likely spend the next 20 years transforming what it means to grow old in America.

- The underlying motivations for today's Boomer Consumer are both natural and a result of their generation's place in time, or Zeitgeist. Marketers should understand how both impact Boomer Consumers.

- Boomers feel some 14 years younger than they actually are. However, that doesn't mean they should be marketed to as if they are actually that age. What they are in their heads – their mental age – probably doesn't match their needs as a consumer.

Chapter 2
Boomer Psychology

W hen actress Rosanna Arquette was making her documentary "Searching for Debra Winger" (2002), she ran into actress Frances McDormand in a ladies' room at a restaurant in France. She filmed the encounter, explaining to McDormand that the subject of her movie was actresses, their love for their art, the tug of war between career and family, and the horrors of getting older in Hollywood, especially for women.

McDormand, who was in her mid-40's at the time, revealed her plan for cosmetic surgery: Not having it. In ten years, she said, "Stories will need to be told about 54-year-old women, but there aren't going to be any women who look 54." So she'd get all the roles.

McDormand had it figured out. Hollywood may start reflecting America, which is now ready for stories about 54-year-olds. Understanding Boomer psychology will help you see why.

Introduction: The Psychology of Aging

Over the past 40 years Boomer Consumers have been labeled the "Youth Generation." And for four decades, that's been true. But what will happen when they hit 50 and beyond? What will be an apt descriptor?

If you take a close look at the basic psychology of aging you'll begin to understand the mindset of older Boomers. This chapter explores the psychology of aging and how it applies to today's Boomer Consumer.

In the Boomer Project's national study we ask a series of questions to learn more about the current mindset of older Boomers, including the following:

> *"They say you're as old as you feel. How old do you feel?"*

Our goal is to assess how many years younger (or older) one feels psychologically as compared to their chronological age. Not surprisingly, Boomers over the age of 50 told us, on average, that they feel some 14 years younger than they are. That means a typical Boomer Consumer over 50, say age 54 or 55, actually feels 40 or 41.

At first glance, you might conclude that the "Youth Generation" label still applies.

In truth, a problem arises when we report this statistic to marketers. They immediately say "that's why we keep targeting young adults between 18-49. Those 54 or 55-year-old Boomers still feel 40, so they can relate to the advertising targeted to 18-49- year-olds."

Our reply to those marketers is that they are *wrong*. While someone in their mid-fifties may still feel young, in their early 40's in this case, that doesn't mean that's where they are *mentally* in their lives. Psychologically, they are much more mature at 54 than they were at 40. In fact, they are different people than when they were 40.

Let us explain.

Developmental psychologists study human growth and development. Most of the focus of study is on how children grow and develop from birth to adulthood. The changes from birth to age 20 are obvious in part because of visible changes in the physical growth. Yet once we reach adulthood, we don't stop our psychological development. It continues from age 20 until death. What is important to us changes over time, as our view of the world grows and changes.

Think about yourself. Are you the same person you were 15 years ago? Are the things that were important to you then, especially in regards to your behavior as a consumer, still important today? Or have they changed?

In October 2004 actress Jamie Lee Curtis was interviewed by *More* magazine and agreed, at age 44, to pose in a two-piece bathing suit to replicate a photograph taken of her at age 24. The "now and then" 44-year-old version was understandably thicker in certain places and sagging in others. She also posed for the new shot without make-up, so age lines and wrinkles were evident.

Caremark Rx :: Mike Critelli/Pitney Bowes :: Larry Culp/Danaher :: Curt Culver/MGIC Investment :: Paul Cur-

In the article she admitted than she had fought growing older throughout most of her thirties, but by the time she reached her early 40's she was comfortable with the fact that she simply wasn't the same person she had been at 24. She was different, and that was just fine.

Most Boomer Consumers have come to the same realization. They may "feel" 35 or 40, but they know they are not that same person. What's important to them and how they view the world has grown and evolved.

The Four Stages of Life

Many developmental psychologists believe that most people who live 80 or more years go through four stages of life. Each lasts about 20 years and consists of Youth, Young Adult, Middle Age, and Senior. Others use the "Seasons" analogy – Spring, Summer, Fall and Winter. Whatever the label, someone between 40 to 60 is in a different place psychologically than they were at 20 to 40.

The "seasons of life" is hardly a recent concept, as exemplified by this old Irish proverb:

> *Twenty years a child;*
> *Twenty years running wild;*
> *Twenty years a mature man;*
> *And after that, praying.*

Understanding the seasons of life is important to marketers for two reasons. First, Boomer Consumers were 42-60 years old as of the end of 2006. As a generation, they are firmly entrenched in life's third quarter — the Fall season, Middle Age. They simply aren't "Young" anymore. And they know it, although marketers may not. Second, "Fall" consumers have different underlying motivations for their behavior than when they were younger.

David Wolfe, in his book *Ageless Marketing*, and on his ongoing blog agelessmarketing.typepad.com, provides a thorough discussion of the scholarly and scientific evidence about the "Seasonal" changes. As he explains it, the first twenty years of one's life, "Spring," is all about initial personal development, learning things through play and a view of the world that everything will generally work out in their favor.

So when you hear an 8-year-old announce that "I'm going to be an astronaut," or "I'm going to be President," or "I'm going to play for the Boston Red Sox," it's perfectly acceptable. Anything is possible during those first 20 years or so, and nearly everyone dreams big.

The next season, "Summer," lasts from about 20-40, and we focus on social and vocational development in our attempt to "become someone" personally and professionally. For many of us, our work or job defines who we are. At this stage, according to Wolfe, we still have a romantic view of the world – "I'm going to run this company someday," or "I'm going to own a vacation home at the beach." We tend to judge ourselves through the eyes of others, and our behavior is influenced more by outwardly-driven or social motivations.

The "Fall" season is from 40-60 or so and the focus for most people now moves towards becoming more inner-directed and self-focused. Rather than being self-absorbed, this shift involves seeking self-respect and self-fulfillment. Wolfe cites Abraham Maslow's "Hierarchy of Needs" which says that the ultimate goal of man (or woman) is to reach self-actualization. It is during this twenty-year period that one typically heads down that path.

Wolfe says that consumers between 40-60 are looking to strike a balance between work and the rest of life. They have come to grips with the reality that they never had the right stuff to be an astronaut, don't want to be President, or couldn't hit a curve ball even if the Red Sox came calling. (A select few, however, did achieve those goals.) Many have come to realize they'd rather spend time with their families and friends than be the boss of the company. They may be never able to afford a beach house but they might be able to swing payments on an RV.

Our research at the Boomer Project has borne out the findings of Wolfe and others. We've seen that, at some point between 40-60, one stops

Charles Davidson/Noble Energy :: Ronald DeFeo/Terex :: Chad Deaton/Baker Hughes :: Claiborne Deming/

concentrating so much on trying to "become someone" and instead focuses on "being someone." Life becomes more about the journey and less about the destination. Marketers need to understand this shift, because the "large and in charge" Boomer generation is now at this "Fall" stage of life.

The final stage, "Winter" is also about reconciliation, trying to make sense out of life and what it all means. Most consumers over 60 have gotten comfortable with who they are (and aren't) and are not likely to be swayed by what others think.

In conclusion, the underlying motivation for consuming behavior in the second half of life, from age 40 onward, is more inner-directed and less socially driven. For example, when a 25-year-old buys a BMW, the motivation is mostly outward, because of what the purchase tells others about them. They see it as a badge announcing that they've "arrived" to their friends, family and co-workers. But when a 55-year-old buys a BMW, the incentive is more inward, and deals with what it tells them about themselves. What matters is how it makes <u>them</u> feel; they don't care nearly as much about what it says to others.

Boomer Insights?

Two recent studies help illuminate the difficulty of trying to figure out the Boomer marketplace.

First, Ameriprise recently released the "New Retirement Mindscape" study which provides insight into the five emotional stages one passes through regarding retirement. They've identified each stage, from 15 years before retirement day to 15 years after.

Stage 1 starts 15 years prior to "Retirement Day" and is called "Imagination." Stage 2 happens about five years out and is called "Anticipation." "Retirement Day" is still identified as a specific event that takes place, just before Stage 3, "Liberation." One short year after Retirement Day comes Stage 4, "Reorientation," followed by Stage 5's "Reconciliation."

While interesting, we aren't sure it is that helpful in trying to determine what emotions Boomers will endure (enjoy?) during their retirement years. Why, you ask?

Our opinion is based on the fact that no Boomer is yet 75 years old. Asking a current 75-year-old about his or her retirement years may not be relevant to Boomers today. At every stage of life, Boomers have done things differently than the previous generations. They look at retirement as done by their parents and already know they'll do it differently. Other than that, Boomers today don't know what their "retirement" will be like.

So mapping out the future for Boomers based on the prior generation's behavior and attitudes may not prove more frustrating than illuminating.

On the other hand, the folks at consulting firm Deloitte took a different approach. They studied current Boomer behavior and made predictions about future behavior. Also an inexact science, but one that may prove to be more accurate. You can download their summary report, called "Wealth With Wisdom: Serving the Needs of Aging Consumers" at www.deloitte.com. It calls for companies and organizations to seize the Boomer opportunity by 2008 or miss the boat. If your top management hasn't read it yet, make sure they do.

Connecting With the Right Message

Developmental psychologists understand how changing motivations lead to different consumer behaviors. But many marketers don't even consider the changes, even though obviously purchasing habits shift as well.

In a recent national study at the Boomer Project we explored the relative importance of key values and motivations among consumers of different

Cablevision NY Group :: Peter Dolan/Bristol-Myers Squibb :: James Donald/Starbucks :: Mark Donegan/Preci-

ages. Sure enough, the values of Boomer Consumers under 50 were more socially-focused and similar to those of younger adults. The values of Boomer Consumers over 50 were more inner-directed and driven by self-respect and self-fulfillment. Marketers who can tap into the changing values of older Boomer Consumers will be more likely to tap into their hearts, minds, and wallets than those treating these same Boomers as 40-year-olds.

For example, in 2005 Lincoln Financial, a large financial services company based in Philadelphia, launched a television campaign targeting leading-edge Boomers over 50. The goal was to sell them retirement planning products and services. The TV spots had the tagline, "Hello Future."

One commercial in particular illustrates an understanding of the changing values of Boomers. It begins with a 60-year-old man on top of a snow-capped mountain and gives the impression he's about to go skiing. It quickly cuts to him approaching a group of special needs kids, one of whom is wearing a jacket that says "Adaptive Ski Team." The man then spends his day helping these children ski. That evening he drives in his Range Rover to his expansive home, where his wife brings him a cup of coffee and asks him about his "first day." He replies: "You know, maybe my dad was right. Maybe I do have a future as a ski bum." Then the narrator briefly explains what Lincoln Financial has to offer. But the message is clear.

This commercial exemplifies the need to understand the different values of older Boomers, as compared to younger Boomers and young adults. The hero of the commercial spends his time taking the special needs kids skiing not for what it says to others, but how it makes him feel inside. He's working on "being someone," not "becoming someone."

One of our clients, Genworth Financial, a multibillion dollar insurance and financial services company, has also transformed its advertising campaign to tap into the psychological maturity of older Boomers. From a consumer marketing point of view, they have a very difficult message to convey. For one thing, most consumers find life insurance and related products confusing and dull. Even those in the industry

sion Castparts :: Craig Donohue/Chicago Mercantile :: Chad Dreier/Ryland Group :: Craig Dubow/Gannett ::

admit that rather than being "low interest," life insurance is a "no interest" category.

For another, in most cases, what they sell won't deliver benefits for years to come. And the purchaser is usually dead, or infirm if it's long-term care insurance. Or, if it's a variable annuity, the purchaser is generally retired and no longer earning an income.

For years, Genworth and everyone else in the insurance industry avoided talking about "insurance" and simply communicated that they were large and stable enough to be around for a long, long time. The goal was to make sure that when the financial advisor sold a policy the long-term security of the purchase was not an issue.

The Boomer Project conducted some educational seminars about today's Boomer Consumer for Genworth, helping them better understand that Boomers are now in the Fall of their lives. Shortly thereafter Genworth undertook an initiative to revamp and build a meaningful brand position for Boomers, centered around the idea that "you're going to live a long time, so you'd better plan for it."

The first element was a TV and print campaign focusing on people who are 100 or more years old. These mini-documentaries present centenarians doing everything from playing the trumpet to attending family picnics. In one commercial, the woman says she had no idea she would live this long.

This campaign provides another example of how a commercial can connect with Boomers 50 and older. They are mature enough to relate to it psychologically; most realize that, all things being equal, they have a pretty good chance at living another 35-40 years. Seeing someone who has done so with style, dignity and vitality is a compelling and motivating message. Hopefully, this is the beginning of a new marketing trend.

BoomBox

The Greater Generation?

Leonard Steinhorn's book, The Greater Generation, poses interesting questions about Boomers and their parents, the so-called Greatest Generation.

The elevator version: Boomers have changed society and culture for the better, something, Steinhorn says, their parents never did. Boomers embraced Civil Rights, gave women rights and equal opportunities, became tolerant of gays and other races and religions, changed business and industry from authoritative to democratic structures, and became stewards of the environment.

We contacted Professor Steinhorn to see what the feedback has been — anticipating that those GI Generation proponents and Baby Boomer opponents would take him to task. Here's what he told us:

"Most gratifying to me is how positive the reaction has been. I've gotten hundreds of e-mails and letters, and a good three-fourths say that the book speaks to them both culturally and personally. Some - - particularly those working in nonprofits or other social change work — say that my book puts their lives and pursuits in a larger generational perspective, that they're not so alone in what they've done. Some — mostly women and minorities - - share their own stories of braving the old attitudes and being thankful for the new.

"Some even say that I've helped them better understand their relationship with their parents. Some are members of the Greatest Generation who thank me for saying what life was really like back then — and who praise me for crediting Boomers for making it better. Some are from Gen X and Y, who have only good things to say about their Boomer elders or parents. And some simply enjoy how I capture the generational zeitgeist.

Centex :: Raymond Elliott/Zimmer Holdings :: Gregg Engles/Dean Foods :: Charlie Ergen/EchoStar Commun ::

"What unifies these messages is gratitude that someone is finally giving Boomers credit for the accomplishments we've made — accomplishments that are too often taken for granted, as if the world were always this way. Most Boomers are simply tired of the popular caricature that we're no more than a bunch of selfish narcissists.

"On the whole, the response has been quite affirming — from all age groups, backgrounds, perspectives. I've even had former Republican speechwriters and World War II veterans thanking me. I expected some controversy, and sure enough it's come. But I don't let the shrill minority bother me because the critical mass has been grateful that I've articulated something that many felt but didn't really know how to express."

It's a Boomer story that's stirring the pot, instead of another one about Boomers smoking pot.

Summary

- Boomers may have been the "Youth Generation" and may still "feel" about 40, but they are psychologically in their "Fall," or life's third quarter. They are no longer young adults, nor are they "Seniors."

- The underlying motivations for behavior in today's Boomer Consumer are inwardly-driven. Rather than being interested in the social payoff of an offering, they're more concerned with how it makes them feel about themselves.

- Boomer Consumers today are more focused on "being someone" than "becoming someone." Rather than being driven by outside forces or friends' opinions, they are trying to find self-fulfillment and self-respect.

Mark Ernst/H&R Block :: Mike Eskew/United Parcel Service :: Bob Essner/Wyeth :: Rich Fairbank/Capital One

Chapter 3
Boomer Sociology

son Electric :: Thomas Farrell/Dominion Resources :: Steven Farris/Apache :: Don Felsinger/Sempra Energy ::

For the last 40 years, if a marketer knew someone's age, they knew a lot about them. That isn't the case today. Scott Thornhill, Matt's brother, is 50. Matt is 47. Demographically they're the same age. Scott has just seen his youngest son start his first year of college. He sold his house and moved into an "empty nester" home in an age-restricted neighborhood. Recently, when his wife entertained out-of-town girlfriends, Scott flew to Detroit for the weekend to attend the International Auto Show, pretty much on a whim. Scott is excited about having the kids in college, which frees him up to work on his golf game and travel.

However, Matt won't be doing the same things as Scott anytime soon. For one thing, Matt has a two-year-old daughter, Mia, and will join the ranks of "empty nesters" around 2023, when Mia goes to college. Matt's neighborhood is full of children in elementary school, and weekends are spent running the kids from one activity to another. Scott's neighbors are all older and weekends don't even include yard work, because the community provides that service as part of his monthly dues. So despite being essentially the same age, Matt and Scott are at two very distinct and different life stages of life.

The days of knowing where someone is in life simply by their age are gone. To understand Boomer Consumers today, we have to better understand their sociology; that is, how they are living their lives.

Introduction: Consumer Sociology 101

Marketing to consumers at different ages used to be fairly easy. Age was an efficient and short-handed way to determine where the consumer was in life, and what products and services they might need.

And in some cases, this is still true today. For example, if someone is 23 years old, we can safely assume they are fresh out of college, unmarried, with an entry-level job or position. So they probably aren't making a ton of money. They live at home, or in an apartment, probably with roommates. They drive a small, sporty car and frequent bars and other places where other young adults hang out. They buy multiple pairs of jeans, drink the same beer as their friends, own an iPod, eat out frequently, go the movies often and don't spend much money at the supermarket.

Brian Ferguson/Eastman Chemical :: Trevor Fetter/Tenet Healthcare :: Jeff Fettig/Whirlpool :: Joseph Ficalora/

If someone is 33, he or she is likely married, has bought a house, probably has one or two small children and may even drive a minivan… to make frequent trips to the supermarket. They eat out less frequently, and usually at a restaurant that ends in an apostrophe "s" — Wendy's, Chili's, TGI Friday's, Applebee's, or Fuddrucker's. The person has a middle management job, a hefty credit card balance, and now drinks wine more often than beer. Movies are usually watched at home, thanks to Blockbuster and Netflix.

Skip ahead to someone who is 53. In the past, they would have had kids in college or out of the house altogether. They were at their peak earning years, in their top position at work. Their debt had been paid down so they had more disposable income than ever before. They ate out regularly, at nicer restaurants. They rarely watched movies, but did go to sporting events and the theatre.

You can see, then, that all marketers really needed to know was someone's age in order to know where they were on life's path.

What made this true for the last 40 years or so has been the fact that the G.I. (1905-25) and Silent (1926-45) Generations lived fairly linear lives. The first 20 years or so were about education; then they would marry and start a job, both of which they kept until death, or in the case of the job, until age 65. They would have kids while in their 20's, when they bought their first house. As they had more kids, they'd move to a second home and then stay in that home until they retired to Florida. So to market to them, all you really needed to know was their age.

Boomers and Roads Taken (or Not)

But Boomers have diverged from that path. They went to college, then stopped, switched schools, or went on and got postgraduate degrees. If they married in their early 20's, over half of them later divorced, and then remarried. They started a job, quit, went to another company, then relocated to a different city, and so on. Five or ten years into their careers, some decided to switch to something else, went back to school, and started all over again. Kids didn't happen until their late 20's or early 30's, and sometimes later than that.

In general, one could conclude, and others have written entire books about it, that rather than following linear paths, Boomers have had *cyclical lives*. They've been doing it since entering adulthood and don't seem to appear to be stopping anytime soon.

This poses quite a problem for marketers who traditionally use age as a shorthand identifier for life stage. Especially since most Boomers are approximately 40-60 and information on their age provides few clues as to where they are in their lives.

In a Boomer Project study, we asked Boomers to select from a list of life stage labels that describe where they right now. Here's what Boomers over 50, for example, told us:

Question: Which of these descriptors would you say relate to you and your life right now?

Parent	50%
Empty Nester	73%
Grandparent	41%
Care-Giver	28%
Retired	26%
New Job	17%
Child in College	20%
Child at Home	27%

Source: Boomer Project National Study, December 2004

Their answers were all over the map. Half say "Parents" is a descriptor that relates to their life right now, and yet nearly three-quarters state "Empty Nester" is accurate. Huh? It seems that in order to have an empty nest now, at one point you had to have had children, which means you're likely still a parent. But we asked the question about "your life right now" and obviously there are Boomer parents with kids out of the house who therefore don't see themselves currently in the role of "parent." We suspect psychiatrists could have a field day with that finding!

The broader point is that today's Boomers can be at many life stages. They could be empty nesters, or they could be parents with young children. Although Matt and his brother Scott are demographically the same age, they are at two completely different life stages. This is quite common among Boomers.

If you're a Boomer, consider your own life. Has it followed a linear path or have there been cycles? How does your life's path compare to that of your parents? What about your Boomer friends? Know any Boomers over 50 with children under the age of five? There's a good chance you probably do.

These cycles create a big issue for marketers, who relied on age as the great short cut in predicting consumer behavior. *With today's Boomer Consumer, age is simply not as relevant as life stage.*

Think of the financial services marketers who target "50-somethings" with messages about retirement planning. It simply isn't relevant for the entire group: Some are still saving to pay for their children's education, while others are embarking on new jobs and careers and retirement is the last thing on their minds. Marketing to consumers between ages 40-60 is much more complicated than in the past.

Twenty years ago, bank marketers could target consumers "over 50" and pitch them "Golden" checking accounts and other services. Everyone "over 50" was at essentially the same life stage and would find the attributes of the product a good fit. No fees. Free checks. A simple statement because those folks "over 50" would likely get all confused dealing with complicated bank records. Looking back at the product descriptions today, they seem insulting.

Today, however, no single checking account product is appropriate for all people "over 50." A 54-year-old Boomer, married the second time, with kids in college from his or her first marriage, and a ten-year-old from the second, would most certainly have different financial services

ee/Sprint Nextel :: Doug Foshee/El Paso :: Michael Fraizer/Genworth Financial :: Lew Frankfort/Coach :: Tom requirements for the checking account than, for example, the Boomer's 84-year-old mother who lives in the spare bedroom.

Marketers who continue to base their messages on someone's age, especially today's Boomers, will likely miss their mark. The age of the target is nice to know, but no longer a solid starting point.

Target Life Stages

Successful marketers use life stages as a way to get Boomers' attention and win them over. For example, part of the "Priceless" series of print ads from MasterCard shows a young boy climbing over a fence. All you see are his legs and about half of his torso, while the rest of him is already leaning over, out of view. The headline says "Indestructible GAP hoodie [sweatshirt] for grandson, $29.50. (Knowing you're not the one who has to wash it, priceless.)"

The beauty of the ad is that while clearly targeting readers with grandkids, it actually doesn't show the grandparents. This is smart because Boomer grandparents don't think of themselves as "old" or grandparent-like. Some 20-something art director's or designer's take on a Boomer grandparent might result in a Wilford Brimley clone. Most Boomer grandparents see themselves more in the category of actor Pierce Brosnan, himself a 50-something grandfather of two.

Some 41% of Boomers over 50 are grandparents. Like parenthood, it's a stage you never leave, and thus a potential gold mine for marketers. Mary Furlong, founder of Third Age, calls the grandparent life stage "the dessert of life" for Boomers. She reminds us that Boomers are the ones who put "Baby on Board" stickers on their minivans because they were so proud of their kids. One can only imagine what Boomers will do for their grandkids.

The grandparent life stage opens up a wide range of marketing opportunities in connecting with today's Boomers. Restaurants looking to attract "early bird" Boomers and their grandkids could develop

Freston/Viacom :: Mike Fries/Liberty Global :: Richard Fuld/Lehman Bros Holdings :: Tom Gallagher/Genuine

special menus and activities for both. Already theme and amusement parks and state fairs have begun selling "grandparent" admission tickets that cost less. Although grandparents won't be on as many of the rides as the grandkids, they'll more than make up the difference by spending oodles of cash on souvenirs, games, and food.

Marketers have also started to feature the "empty nest" life stage in their advertisements as a way to target and reach Boomers. It's a standard approach in the industry, taking a "slice of the consumer's life" and portraying it in the ad, with the product prominently featured. For decades, thousands of "slice of life" commercials have featured a traditional family of four, with two kids ages 5-15.

But now we're starting to see "slice of life" commercials with no kids, or with college-aged kids. These ads are clearly targeting older Boomers now in the empty-nest life stage.

In a TV commercial for Lowe's Home Improvement, a college-aged son returns home with a duffle bag of dirty laundry, only to find the washing machine and dryer on the curb as trash. He's relieved when he sees there is a Lowe's truck in the driveway, unloading a new washer and dryer. Mom and Dad tousle his hair and give him a hard time about only coming home to do his laundry. The announcer then espouses the great deals at Lowe's, and tells us they'll deliver and install appliances.

Cute commercial, and effective in targeting Boomers with college-aged kids. Like many commercials, this one relies on a "slice of life" to get the audience's attention, using a life stage that *the majority* of their potential customers can relate to. The new consumer majority, as David Wolfe calls them in his book *Ageless Marketing*, are those consumers over the age of 40. The point is to depict a "slice of life" that most of your consumers will find real and believable, and most importantly, relevant.

Conversely, if you want to appeal to today's Boomers, you probably may not want to show pregnant moms or infants in your commercials or print ads, unless they are expectant offspring or grandkids, respectively.

Parts :: Jay Gellert/Health Net :: Robert Genader/Ambac Financial Group :: Vincent Gierer/UST :: Ken Glass/

Most Boomers are past that life stage and are not as likely to relate to those situations.

We'll talk more about this in Chapter 13, but the point is: Today's Boomer Consumer can be best targeted by life stage, not age.

What a Difference a Day Makes
Christopher Bonney, Bonney Research

I turned fifty-five the other day. I didn't think too much of it. I was still doing all the same things I'd been doing twenty-four hours earlier when I was fifty-four. I didn't feel older. I didn't feel marginalized. And I certainly didn't feel insulted.

That didn't happen until later in the day.

It all started with a research survey. The afternoon of my 55th birthday I received an invitation to take part in an online survey. When asked for my age, I put my check in the "55-64" box and immediately screened out of the survey.

I didn't think much of it at first. Then I got another invitation to take part in another online survey and I screened out of that one, too, right after I checked the "55 – 64" box. And then it happened again on yet another survey later in the day.

I started wondering whether because of my age my opinions no longer mattered. Then I started noticing other, more subtle ways I was becoming marginalized by the marketplace. I noticed how many commercials and ads for products I buy regularly never show anyone in them who looks anywhere near my age or, if they do, how they seem to think that men in their fifties have nothing more pressing to think about than playing golf or, for women, how they're going to handle the embarrassment of crow's feet or incontinence.

First Horizon National :: Larry Glasscock/WellPoint :: Russell Goldsmith/City National :: Hugh Grant/Monsanto ::

One morning this week I saw commercials for one of the nation's most popular tourist destinations that included only one person among twenty or so featured who appeared to be over the age of thirty-five. What a strange condition, I thought, in a country where people over 45 make up such a large part of the population and Baby Boomers specifically make up the most affluent travel segment?

Am I just feeling the sting of middle age? Do I really have more in common with people ten years older than me than I do with people one day younger? Am I supposed to take my Jimi Hendrix records and just fade into the background?

When I first started doing marketing research among older Americans, a common complaint I heard was:

> *"I wish people wouldn't define me by my age. I may be seventy-two years old, but that's not who I am. The things that describe me and my life and my relationships with other people are the values and experiences we have in common. Except for a few medical things, maybe, age is nothing about who I am."*

Of course age isn't who we are. But it's been the most common means for segmenting consumers for the last sixty years. It's just taken me until age of fifty-five to realize that age was neither the right, nor even a necessarily accurate way to classify people.

At best, age is a coincident measure. What defines us more, and more accurately, are the conditions of our upbringing. As individuals and generations, we are reflections of our times, not of time itself. The "times" which shaped us have only rarely been defined by a uniform interval of years and they have certainly not always come in neat ten-year increments.

So where does this all intersect with me turning fifty-five?

As a researcher, I'm going to start looking at new ways of classifying people who do not use age as a primary factor. I want to develop a segmentation model based not just on "where we were

Barry Griswell/Principal Financial :: Raj Gupta/Rohm and Haas :: Jim Hackett/Anadarko Petroleum :: Brian Halla/

when," to borrow Morris Massey's term, but to look at who we are now and how we want to be in the years to come.

For marketers who want to connect with Baby Boomers, success is going to come from connecting with people based on who they are, how they live, what challenges they face in their daily lives and what they aspire to be rather than on some artificial chronological measuring stick. Success will come not just from using popular 1960s rock anthems in advertising, but rather from tapping into the emotions, experiences and values that made such songs meaningful to us and that continue to shape who we are today.

Life Style Matters, Too

For years, marketers have segmented their audience by life style factors as well. Things like income, education, job, geography, political persuasion, religion and other "soft" factors can be used to draw distinctions among consumers. The 78 million Boomers born between 1946-64 come in about 78 million different sizes, colors, creeds and income levels. They aren't a single segment, in fact, some demographers state they consist of two cohorts, roughly split between 1946-1954 and 1955-1964. (This will be discussed in the next chapter).

Merrill Lynch conducted a large study of the Boomer cohort in 2005 and came up with five distinct segments:

- Empowered Trailblazers
- Wealth-Builders
- Leisure Lifers
- Anxious Idealists
- Stretched and Stressed

Another firm, JWT Mature Market Group (www.jwtmmg.com), published a report on the 40+ consumer today separating them into 24 distinct segments:

Conservative Elites	Rustic Retirees
Gold 'n Gray	Urban Ethnic Blend
Metro Influentials	American Bedrock
Urban Elegance	Urban Strugglers
Sunset Blues	Classic Rockers
Senior Suburbia	Independent Spirits
Urban Sophisticates	Liberal Achievers
Standard-Bearers	Small Town Living
Elder Sages	Southern Traditionalists
Middle Class Empty Nesters	Small Town Traditionalists
Rural Family Values	Blue Collar Boomers
American Dreamers	Mainstream Matures

JWT based the differences between each segment on:

- Purchasing power and behavior
- Lifestyle choices
- Values
- Demographic attributes
- Socio-economic status
- Attitudes

Focalyst Research (www.focalyst.com), a marketing firm affiliated with AARP Services, identified and quantified six distinct segments among the population of those people ages 42 and up (the 78 million Boomers, and the 47 million Americans age 61 and up). They labeled their segments, and revealed the relative size of each:

- Overwhelmed and Unfortunate   25%
- Active and Successful   24%
- Positive and Responsible   20%
- Regular Folk   16%
- Fortunate and Ready   14%
- Alone and Ill   2%

We're not sure what all this segmenting of the Boomer cohort ultimately means to most marketers (Who is going to put much effort towards "Overwhelmed and Unfortunate" and "Alone and Ill"?). But these three studies emphasize the fact that Boomers aren't a single segment. They

Hanway/Cigna :: Eli Harari/SanDisk :: Brett Harvey/Consol Energy :: Fred Hassan/Schering-Plough :: Pat Has-

consist of many different segments and thus can't all consume and be marketed to the same way.

Many marketers have already begun segmenting in an attempt to identify the best prospects. This needs to continue as you think about targeting today's Boomer Consumer. Factors such as income, education, geography and more need to be considered in finding the best audience for your product.

Our advice: Put age on the back burner. Or, as they used to say in the 1960s, it's irrelevant.

Hollywood Comes of Age?

At the beginning of Chapter 2, we discussed an encounter between actresses Frances McDormand and Rosanna Arquette during the making of documentary "'Searching for Debra Winger," (2002). In it, McDormand stated that she had no plans for plastic surgery because in ten years there would be a demand for actresses who actually looked their age.

Actress Teri Garr, who is also in her 50's, hopes she's right. "There are people that are my age and older that still exist in the world," she says, and writers who write about them. "So there must be parts for us." You'd think.

"Searching for Debra Winger" asks timeless questions about women and aging. Arquette, the director, interviewed famous subjects such as Gwyneth Paltrow, Meg Ryan, Vanessa Redgrave, Sharon Stone, Melanie Griffith, Daryl Hannah, Ally Sheedy, Whoopi Goldberg, Jane Fonda, and Diane Lane.

"People started to ask me when I was like 35, are you worried that you're not going to work anymore?" wonders Griffith, now in

sey/Allegheny Technologies :: Ron Havner /Public Storage :: Lewis Hay/FPL Group :: Rob Henrikson/MetLife ::

her late 40's. Hannah, a few years younger, says people were shocked to learn she was playing a teenager's mother.

Hollywood, like Madison Avenue, loves youth and lionizes the young. Or at least that was the case for the last 40 years. But the success of Jack Nicholson and Diane Keaton in the 2004 film "Something's Got to Give" spawned a new era. More and more movies featuring (gasp!) maturing actors and actresses dealing with later-in-life issues are beginning to grace cineplexes everywhere. In fact, in 2005, the movie "Sideways" won critical acclaim and scored well at the box office. They topic was two single, middle aged men on one last weekend romp in wine country before an upcoming marriage. People under 40 probably didn't even understand the movie, and audiences over 40 loved it.

Hollywood is showing signs of a new consumer majority, where actresses like Frances McDormand, with her unaltered face, will likely continue to land starring roles no matter her age.

Summary

While it once was critical that a marketer know the target audience's ages, such is not the case with today's Boomers, who are between 40-60. Age is simply not revealing enough to be a good starting point. Some Boomers at 54 have children under 10 while others at 44 who have offspring in college.

A better starting point in targeting Boomers would be by life stage. Do they have kids at home? What are the ages of the children? Are they empty nesters? Grandparents? Understanding the household composition provides more clues about the products and services that a Boomer family will want and need.

Marketers that target a life style will also have success in reaching today's Boomer Consumer. Overall, segmenting Boomers by anything other than their actual age is a better place to start.

Ron Hermance /Hudson City Bancorp :: John Hess/Amerada Hess :: Steve Heyer/Starwood Hotels :: Vern Hill /

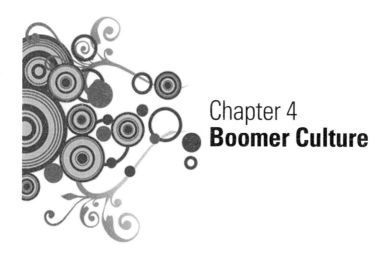

Chapter 4
Boomer Culture

A
nn Dempsey is a 56-year-old Boomer, the oldest of six children and now the mother of two 20-somethings. Ann moved a dozen times with her parents during her first 20 years, as dad Arthur worked as a manager for the K-Mart Corporation, opening new stores as the company expanded across the Northeast. Ann spent her childhood in homes in various suburban outposts across New York, New Jersey, Pennsylvania and Connecticut. Each one was essentially like the other, and her dad always brought home K-Mart's newest products, from iron to the toaster oven to color TV. She spent her "Wonder Bread years" among the latest and greatest gadgets and modern conveniences.

Ann found that the easiest way to connect with the other kids in her new school was by talking about what she'd seen on television. This provided a foundation for shared experiences which developed into friendships.

By the time Ann was a sophomore accounting major at Syracuse University, she had friends who had been drafted to fight in Vietnam, never to return. She protested against the war on campus and met her soon-to-be-husband and father of her two children.

Ann doesn't put much thought into those first 20 or so years of her life, from 1950 to approximately 1970. Yet they shaped her and made her who she is today. Demographers recognize her "cohort" because of her place in time and history. But most marketers don't fully appreciate the importance of that shared history and experience.

Introduction: Boomer Influence

It's been said that the first half of one's life is shaped by the history they experience and the second half is when they shape history. Think about it. Boomers today are in the second half of their lives and indeed are shaping their own history.

William Jefferson Clinton was the first Boomer generation President, followed by George W. Bush. We'll likely have Boomer-aged Presidents for the next 20 or more years. Supreme Court Justice Clarence Thomas

Humann/SunTrust Banks :: Peter Huntsman/Huntsman :: Mark Hurd/Hewlett-Packard :: Sanford Ibrahim/Radian

was the first Boomer selected to the highest court in the land, and just recently he was joined by fellow Boomers Chief Justice John Roberts and Justice Samuel Alito. Over time, most if not all the justices will be Boomers.

Although Boomers may comprise only 33% of the over-21 population in America, consider the following:

- In Congress, of the 435 members elected in 2006 317 are Boomers (70%).

- Of the CEOs of the Fortune 500 companies, some 80% or 399 are Boomers.

- Winners of the last ten Best Actor, Actress and Director categories, 30 total awards, were collected 15 times by Boomers. And this is in youth-obsessed Hollywood!

The Boomer generation is large and in charge of American politics, business and culture. But how did they get there? And what did they experience during the first half of their lives and how did that affect them?

The Beginning

Demographers believe that what separates one generation from another is essentially each generation's unique place in time and history. American Baby Boomers, born between 1946-64, grew up in one time and place, while Generation X, born from 1965-82 had different experiences. The same is true of Generation Y or the Millennials. However, recent immigrants who may be the same age as American Boomers may not connect with them because they grew up in another country or culture and thus don't share the same history.

Demographers also state that experiences from the generation's first 20 years or so shape its social and personal mores, values and traits. Consider, for example, the G.I. and the Silent Generations, which grew up during the Great Depression and World War II, respectively. Those events had significant impact on how each generation views the world, their sense of duty, how they manage money and many other personal values.

Group :: Bob Iger/Walt Disney :: Jeff Immelt/General Electric :: Susan Ivey/Reynolds American :: Mike Jackson/

If you're a Boomer, what experiences and events had an impact on your views and values during your "Wonder Bread years"? For most, the list is long and includes things like the birth of television, the threat of the atomic bomb and the Cold War, the launch of Sputnik and the start of the space race, the birth of rock 'n roll, Kennedy's Camelot, Kennedy's assassination, Civil Rights, Martin Luther King Jr., Vietnam, Nixon, Watergate, *All in the Family*, disco and so on.

Understanding the Boom

There is much to understand about those shared experiences and what they mean for today's Boomer Consumer. In many respects, the experts were caught off-guard by the Baby Boom. While they predicted an increase in births following World War II, it was nothing like what they expected.

For the better part of the previous 140 years, the birth rate in America had been steadily declining, from about seven to three babies per woman. This shift towards smaller families took place as America went from a nation of farmers to an urban, industrial country, focusing the shift from needing a large number of children who would provide the necessary physical labor to maintain the farm to fewer mouths to feed. For many factory workers, more children were an economic liability, requiring food, clothes and shelter with little contribution expected in return.

During the Depression and World War II, people put off having children. But nine months after August 15, 1945, VJ day, the Baby Boom began. Starting in early 1946 and over the next 19 years, the typical American woman had four babies, with the Boom peaking in 1957-58 when a new baby arrived every eight seconds. For those keeping track, the birth rate dropped in 1965, signaling the end of the "Boom." Currently it is now at 2.08 children per woman, or just enough for the United States to maintain its current population (immigration is driving growth).

At the end of World War II there was pent-up demand, if you will, for babies. Couples in their 30's who had postponed marriage and families rushed to get started, while at the same time those in their 20's also began having children. Some scholars also contend that the threat of the Cold War and nuclear competition spurred the growth in marriage and birth rates throughout the 1950s. The thinking is that the Boomer "Mamas and Papas" relied on the comfort of home and hearth to stave off the fear of atomic annihilation. Having lots of babies and raising them to be good citizens seemed to be the best way to win the Cold War.

These Boomer children were, as a result of their place in time and history, bound together as a generation. What connected them more tightly than many other generations were three key factors:

- As a result of WWII, the United States had become the undisputed world power, which created a sense of national pride that was carried forward throughout the 1950s and 60s. Boomer children may have grown up in the Northeast, Southwest and everywhere in-between, but the regional differences took a back seat to the feeling of what it meant to be an "American."

- Television linked these Boomer children through shared experiences. Never before had anyone been able to see, hear and experience things at the same time as they could through television. It provided a new and unprecedented level of connectedness.

- Parenting became more standardized, due, in good part to Dr. Benjamin Spock's *The Common Sense Book of Baby and Child Care*. It was published in 1946, the first year of the Baby Boom. A study in 1961 found that two-thirds of all new mothers had read this book which instructed parents to go light on punishment and heavy on reason and persuasion, and that their children's happiness was the top objective. Spock made permissive or child-centered parenting mandatory for millions of postwar middle-class families.

The Boomers were also raised during a time of unbridled economic prosperity and the birth and growth of suburbia. Living on Dad's salary alone, the parents of Boomers were able to buy a home, one or two cars, a TV and all sorts of modern "automatic" appliances and conveniences.

:: Jeff Joerres/Manpower :: John Johns/Protective Life :: Greg Johnson/Franklin Resources :: William Johnson/

Mom stayed home and nurtured the children, who formed the core of the family. As journalist Joshua Zeitz wrote in *American Heritage* magazine, Boomers were "taught to value their needs and satisfy their wants, and imbued with a sense of national greatness and purpose, it would have been odd had they not entered young adulthood without at least some sense of entitlement."

Boomer Traits

Knowing this, we can perhaps start to get a better sense of what these shared early experiences mean to today's Boomer Consumer. The GI's returning after WWII earned the "Greatest Generation" moniker due to their sense of honor, duty and responsibility in stopping Nazism and Fascism. But the America they came back to was pretty much a closed society. Women rarely worked outside of the home and didn't have equal rights. For example, if they were married, depending upon the circumstances, they might not have been able to have a credit card in their own name. Blacks and other minorities were second-class citizens. There was little concern for the environment. Corporate executives ran roughshod over employees. Sexual orientation wasn't a topic of any conversation, much less polite discussion.

Over the last 40 years, much of that has changed, thanks in large part to Boomers. Boomers may not have led the changes in society — Gloria Steinem is a Silent Generation member, for example — but they have been the legions of followers that have made the changes permanent. We now live in a much more open, tolerant, and forgiving society. Sure, many aspects can stand improvement – an excess of political correctness which can hamper free speech; a culture where everyone is a victim yet no one is responsible. But generally, the pendulum has swung from an oppressive to more open society.

All of those experiences shape generational traits that tend to be found in Boomers. In our work we've identified six distinctive traits that predominate Boomers to this day, all rooted in their shared experiences growing up.

HJ Heinz :: Larry Johnston/Albertsons :: Mike Johnston/Visteon :: John Jones/Air Prods & Chems :: Clay M

1. Entitlement
2. Personal gratification
3. Work ethic
4. Control
5. Optimism
6. Won't accept the status quo

Entitlement and Personal Gratification

As mentioned earlier, the Boomer sense of entitlement is a natural result of their upbringing and time and place in history. The shift towards a child-centered home certainly fed the development of this trait. What probably made it stronger was the fact that as Boomers went through their "Wonder Bread years" everything and everybody adapted to them. Dad and Mom moved to larger homes so they could have their own bedrooms, or at least some privacy. Communities built schools and pools and shopping centers and then malls, providing them with places to learn, play and shop. Restaurants created "Children's Menus" and later, an entirely new concept called "fast food" to capture their fleeting fancy and dollars. Colleges added new subject areas and campuses to attract and appeal to them. Car manufacturers from other countries brought forth smaller, less expensive automobiles. Even television networks remade themselves to draw Boomers in hopes attracting advertisers.

With all this constant attention and focus, Boomers came to see themselves as "large and in charge." They could use their numbers and might to bend virtually any industry or institution to their needs. They have been doing that since they were young children and will keep on doing it until the last one dies.

When it comes to personal gratification, we often joke in our seminars and speeches that the theme song for the Boomer generation ought to be the Rolling Stone's classic "Satisfaction," as in "I can't get no satisfaction." To be honest, it isn't completely the Boomers' doing. Their *parents* helped turn them into big-time consumers seeking personal gratification. Throughout the 1950s and 60s, Mom and Dad bought the latest appliances and gizmos to fill their new suburban houses. With the launch of Bank Americard and other credit cards, conspicuous consumption was born, right under the impressionable eyes of young Boomers.

It's no surprise Boomers became remarkable consumers themselves once they reached adulthood. First, they had been given practically everything they ever had wanted growing up. They had gotten college educations and found themselves to be earning more at age 25 than their fathers made at 35 or older. Plus, once married, they had two incomes, thanks to women's rights and the acceptance of women into the workforce. Let the spending begin!

Naturally Boomers taught their own children, the Millennium Generation, to be über multitasking consumers, but that's a story for another day (and book).

Work Ethic

Yet most Boomers also have a strong work ethic. In fact, Boomers have transformed work in America, thanks in large part to their education and numbers.

In previous generations, blue-collar jobs had been the norm for the middle class. The way to get ahead was to work longer and harder than the next guy, which sometimes meant working a second job or 60 hours a week or more. White-collar employment went to the few with education or family money, and those jobs were an "easy" 40 hour week.

Compared to their parents, a larger percentage Boomers graduated from college (33% compared to 26%). Since there were millions more Boomers than previous generations, that meant a huge increase in educated Boomers from all walks of life seeking professional jobs and careers. Add Boomer women into the mix, whose employment was accepted if not desired, then huge changes in the workplace were afoot.

Faced with numerous and fierce competition, white-collar Boomers figured out that they needed to work longer and harder than the next guy or gal. They realized the path to the top started by paying dues, which required time and commitment. Hence, the creation of the 60+ hour work week for white-collar jobs.

Boomers have seemingly turned the American workplace upside down. Ironically, today only blue-collar jobs seem to require a 40-hour work week. Many white-collar workers toil 60 or more hours. The next two generations, Xers and Millennials, don't seem to be as driven by work as Boomers. Many don't understand why Boomers work such long hours and are so dedicated to their jobs.

For many Boomers, their work is their identity and provides them with a strong sense of self. Rather than their name, home town or even education, their work defines who and what they are. Work is central to their very being.

David Brooks, now a columnist for *The New York Times*, wrote the book *Bobos in Paradise* about class and consumption in America. Brooks, a former reporter for *The Wall Street Journal,* had been stationed in Europe during the 1990s. When he returned to the United States, he was struck by how two seemingly opposite lifestyles had come together in how we consumed things. One was "Bourgeois," or the refined upper class. The other, "Bohemians," consisted of down-to-earth, unpretentious, laid-back types. Brooks came up with "bobos" to describe those who manage to marry these two lifestyles. Most of Brooks' "bobos" are Boomers. Some might argue that most Boomers are "bobos" as well.

According to Brooks, an example of the bobo lifestyle would be renovating one's kitchen, installing a $4,000 Viking Range (Bourgeois), so one can cook organic, free-range chicken (Bohemian). Or the Boomer who buys the $2,000 Cannonade bicycle to attach to their $65,000 Range Rover so they can get "back to nature" and go mountain biking. Another aspect Brooks noticed was how bobos have turned the mundane and commonplace into prestigious and special: the $8 Calvin Klein white tee shirt; the $5 cup of coffee from Starbucks.

In researching his concept, Brooks went back and read the marriage notices in *The New York Times*, comparing the ones from the 1950s to those of the '70s. He discovered that the paper had changed how and what they wrote about the bride, the groom and their backgrounds. In the 1950s it was all about family name and heritage; for example, "Lucy Smith of the Hamptons, daughter of Dr. and Mrs. Harold Smith, granddaughter of Bexley and Harriett Smith, married Jonathan Jones from Croton-on-Hudson, son of ..." and so forth. Status came with the gene pool and practically nothing else mattered.

But by the late 1960s and '70s, however, education, degrees and current employer had replaced family name and heritage. For instance, "Lucy Smith, graduate of Vassar and now with Goldman Sachs, married Jonathan Jones, Harvard undergraduate and Yale Law Degree, currently a lawyer in the general counsel's office at American Express..." Key pedigrees were now education and job.

Those GI Generation middle-class Dads and Moms had succeeded in providing more and better opportunities for their Boomer kids. Status and importance could be earned with a good education and the right job. Over the years, millions of Boomers have proven this time and time again.

No wonder Boomers have transformed the workplace in America. Time will tell if the subsequent generations adopt the Boomer work ethic. Right now they view work as less essential to their core being. It simply doesn't define them as it does for Boomers.

Control

Another trait found in most Boomers is a need to be in control. Back in the 1960s, when Boomers rebelled against "The Establishment" and saw it capitulate to their demands regarding civil and women's rights, leaving Vietnam and other issues, they realized they had control. They've held onto it ever since.

Back then, their music took over the country and ultimately, the world. Their entertainment could be found on TV every night and movie theaters every weekend. Their fashions and tastes, from clothes to food, have dominated the social scene for over 40 years.

Their control is so widespread that there really isn't much of a generation gap between Boomers and their Gen Y children. Except perhaps for rap and grunge, two Gen X inventions, most Gen Y kids like the same music as their parents. Go to any aging rocker reunion tour concert and you'll see Boomers and their kids, singing along with The Eagles or Billy Joel.

Optimism

In survey after survey, Boomers paint a picture of the future with a rose-colored brush, always seeing the glass as half-full. This optimistic life view has much to do with the prosperity of the 1950s and '60s, when they came of age. As a generation, they never had an economic depression nor made the sacrifices required of Americans during World War II (some Boomers, however, braved the front lines of Vietnam as soldiers, while others protested at home, fighting to stop the war or for civil and women's rights). In more recent years, of course, there have been rough times, including terrorism engendered by 9/11 and the situation in the Middle East. But Boomers are living through these events as fully-formed adults, not coming-of-age youngsters. That's why if you ask any Boomer about the future they will, on average, have a positive outlook.

From a marketing standpoint, if you sell your product wrapped in a "gloom and doom" message, it likely won't work with Boomers. Telling a Boomer to save for a rainy day is wasted as they know that the sun will come up tomorrow. In contrast, the parents of Boomers were much more pragmatic and would not respond as well to an upbeat message when a dose of "cold, hard" reality was better suited.

Mark Ketchum/Newell Rubbermaid :: Leo Kiely/Molson Coors Brewing :: Kerry Killinger/Washington Mutual ::

Conversely, we don't as yet know how Gen Y will respond on the positive/ negative scale. On the one hand, their Boomer parents set the example for a positive outlook. On the other, they've grown up during a time of terrorism from abroad and school violence at home. Their psyches and overall outlook are therefore different than Dad's and Mom's.

Won't Accept the Status Quo

As mentioned in Chapter 2, Leonard Steinhorn's book *The Greater Generation* set forth the contributions of Boomers to American culture and society. One trait found in Boomers is a refusal to accept things the way they are and to change them, presumably for the better. Throughout their lives Boomers have participated in tremendous changes in our society. Our culture is quite different today than it was in 1946, when the first Boomer was born.

Knowing that about Boomers, it is likely that the next aspect of American life to be transformed by Boomers is aging itself. Although, in the past, Boomers may have made jokes at the expense of old people — remember the Wendy's commercial from the 1980s with Clara Peller yelling "Where's the beef?" — they won't tolerate it as they become the "old people." Once again, the status quo will be changed because of — and by — the Boomers.

 **Boom**Box

Generation Jones

There is a school of thought that "Baby Boomers" are only those people born between 1946 and 1954. Those born in 1955 through 1964 belong to a separate and unique generation, called "Generation Jones" by author Jonathan Pontell. Pontell, and others, ascribe to the belief that an 18-year time span for a generation is too long. Those Boomers born in 1946 could have their own children born in 1964, so both would technically be Boomers, despite being two different generations.

Recall we said in the last chapter that segmenting Boomers by life stage and life style is better than segmenting them based on age alone. The Generation Jones perspective is that their coming-of-age experiences are very different from the older Boomers, and that in itself, makes them different. Older Boomers came of age in the 1960s and made the short list for service in Vietnam. Generation Jones members came of age in the 1970s and danced to Kool & the Gang and disco, not Elvis.

We don't think it is necessary to argue the finer points of who is a "Boomer" and who is a member of this "Generation Jones." Demographers tell us a generation is typically about 20 years, so we'll stick with that. There are always a front half and a back half to any generation. Boomers, one could say, consists of those who knew where they were when JFK was killed, and those who knew where they were when RFK was killed. Or, put another way, the first half had Bob Dylan and the second half had Bruce Springsteen as their rock hero.

Dylan and Springsteen are different. But the underlying traits that make someone like a Dylan or Springsteen really aren't that different.

A Boomer Archetype?

It is unrealistic to group the 78 million Boomers into one overreaching archetype or as having a single characteristic. We realize that marketers are looking for a shorthand method of understanding today's Boomer Consumer. The following "take" may help, but remember that despite their similarities, all Boomers are unique, and there are as many exceptions as rules.

That being said, although there is no single Boomer archetype they are, on the whole, *Driven, Transformational,* and *"Self" Centered.*

Klappa/Wisconsin Energy :: Bill Klesse/Valero Energy :: Scott Kriens/Juniper Networks :: David Kyle/Oneok ::

- *Boomers are Driven.* Think rock band Queen: "I want it all and I want it now." Boomers want control and they want satisfaction.

- *Boomers are Transformational.* They make change happen; they won't accept the status quo.

- *Boomers are "Self" Centered.* They believe in entitlement and personal gratification. Their main question is, "What's in it for me?" Raised as the center of their home universe, Boomers can thank Dr. Spock (as opposed to "Star Trek's" Mr. Spock) and their parents for this focus on themselves. In comparison, consider latch-key Generation Xers and their self-image. Many had to deal with Mom and Dad working and/or single-parent homes while they were growing up. According to most observers, it is not as much "all about them" as it is for Boomers.

We suggest you only use this framework as a starting point in understanding the large and dynamic Boomer generation. It offers a lens in which you should investigate the other factors that complete the "big picture" of today's Boomer Consumer.

Boomer Culture

In our work, we try to help marketers realize that most Boomers can be reached by tapping into their shared history and culture. Many marketers use the easiest tool: rock 'n roll music. But that isn't necessarily the best. While the popularity of various "Golden Oldies" and "Classic Rock" stations continue, overall there isn't a big nostalgic movement among Boomers at this stage of their lives.

In our research, for example, we asked Boomers what period of their lives was their personal best, or peak. We specifically were interested in what decade was the most significant to them. Our hypothesis was that older Boomers, those over 50, would likely tell us the Sixties. Younger Boomers, those born in 1955 and later, would likely declare the Seventies as the best.

Guess what Boomers actually said?

A surprising number told us they have not as yet reached their peak. They aren't "over the hill" looking back fondly at days gone by. They are still looking forward, up the hill, at things they still want or have to do. Some 33% of Boomers over 50 said they hadn't peaked, as did 40% of those under 50. That means developing a campaign based on nostalgic images or music might be ignored by a third to 40% of your audience simply because they aren't looking backwards at all.

The trick isn't to look backwards but to be contemporary and current.

We Love Mr. Spock

In late 2006 we were quoted in a story in *The New York Times* about how Boomers are being over-scrutinized these days. The reporter wanted to make the case that marketers should already know everything about Boomers, since they've been targeting and researching them for some 40 years. Her contention was that there's nothing new to learn.

Part of our argument was that if that were true, more marketers would be following the lead of pain reliever Aleve and using Boomer cultural icons like "Star Trek's" Mr. Spock in their ads, rather than simply borrowing music from Bob Dylan or the Who. Our own research among today's Boomers suggests that nostalgia has limited appeal, since the majority of Boomers are still in the prime of life, moving forward and not looking back. We recommend our clients avoid nostalgia and instead find relevant cultural icons from when Boomers went through their "Wonder Bread years."

The Aleve spot does just that by featuring actor Leonard Nimoy preparing to go on stage at a Trekkie convention. Turns out his arthritis is acting up, making it painful to make his "live long and

Lauder Companies :: Rick Lenny/Hershey :: Wayne Leonard/Entergy :: Dave Lesar/Halliburton :: Aylin Lewis/

prosper" hand gesture. One Aleve later and he wows the crowd with his signature salute.

At the same time, DirecTV was airing a TV spot using the entire Star Trek bridge crew in uniform, marveling over the high-definition of picture Star Fleet on DirecTV. However, the DirecTV spot relies too much on nostalgia about the old show, instead of simply using the actors in a situation relevant to today, like Aleve did. As illogical as it sounds, we love Mr. Spock!

Earlier in this chapter we referred to the developing years in the lives of Boomers as their "Wonder Bread years." That expression makes perfect sense to our Boomer-aged readers, because it's a cultural reference from their childhood. For our Gen X and Gen Y readers, it refers to an advertising line for Wonder Bread, which "builds strong bodies 8 (and later, 12) ways." The TV commercials used the term "Wonder Bread years" to describe youth and adolescence, the time when growing boys and girls would best benefit from vitamin-laced white bread.

We used the reference intentionally to demonstrate that it is possible to reach out and connect with 78 million Boomers by leveraging their shared experiences. The same can be done with Generation X and Y.

When selling to Boomers, think beyond the Rolling Stones, the Who, Bob Dylan and the Beatles and use your imagination about Boomer culture. There is a lifetime of experiences marketers can draw upon to woe the attention and money of today's Boomer Consumer.

Summary

Boomers are bound together as a generation because of their shared place in time and history. The experiences they had growing up in a post-WWII America shaped their world views, values, sensibilities and formed their "archetype" or characteristics. Marketers can tap into those shared traits and experiences, reaching out and connecting with today's Boomers, who differ vastly from one another on many levels.

Sears Holdings :: Ken Lewis/Bank of America :: Ed Liddy/Allstate :: Carl Lindner/American Financial Group ::

Those traits include:

1. Entitlement
2. Personal gratification
3. Work ethic
4. Control
5. Optimism
6. Won't accept the status quo

As a result, Boomers tend to be Driven, Transformational and "Self" Centered.

Tapping into the Boomer culture is an effective and easy way to connect with today's Boomer Consumers, but it requires more in-depth research and understanding than using classic rock 'n roll music.

Part 2
New Rules for Selling and Marketing to Today's Boomer Consumer

Part 2: Introduction

Part 1 provided a basic understanding of today's Boomer Consumer — who they are, what's going on in their heads and lives, and what relevant aspects of their experiences, from their youth to their culture, matter to them today.

Now the discussion turns to the "New Rules" for selling and marketing to Boomers. These rules are mostly based from our research on today's Boomer Consumer, through national online surveys and questionnaires as well as information obtained through our million-member Boomer panel from Survey Sampling International (SSI, www.surveysampling.com). Thanks to two ongoing studies by BIGresearch (www.bigresearch.com), we've also taken a close look at Boomer behaviors related to media consumption as well as recent and planned purchase activity. The two studies are the Consumer Intentions & Actions study, conducted monthly since 2001 among 7,000+ consumers, and the twice-yearly SIMM study of simultaneous media consumption among 15,000 respondents.

In addition to our own data and that of our strategic partners, we have read, studied and analyzed secondary research related to today's Boomer Consumer. Resources include AARP, MetLife's Mature Marketing Institute, Del Webb's Boomer Real Estate studies and others. They are cited where relevant in the "New Rules."

The "New Rules" are specific and intended to provide guidance to marketers and advertising professionals. The goal is to reach, understand, and clearly communicate your message to today's Boomer Consumer. Along with being practical and tactical, they can be put to use immediately. We will also discuss the underlying theory or data behind each "Rule" which will also help you connect with today's Boomer Consumer.

Chapter 5
Rule 1: Treat Everyone Differently

W*achovia, the financial services giant, runs a newspaper ad that states: "There are perks to being over 50. Our checking account is one of them." The ad then goes on to talk about their "Crown Classic" checking account exclusively designed for consumers age 50+. Product features include free checking as long as the consumer maintains a balance of $1,000, a free safe deposit box, free checks, and two free ATM withdrawals a month from outside the Wachovia network.*

On the surface, this product seems like a good idea – a special configuration for the banking needs of consumers "over 50." With names like "Golden Accounts" that were euphemisms for "senior" and "old," they were developed about 25 years ago as a way to attract senior customers, who, compared to younger adults, had simpler financial needs. Banks wanted older customers because they tended to be savers and not borrows, providing the funds that the bank could then loan out to young families.

Today, however, these products need to be reconfigured. Financial service customers "over 50" are no longer a homogeneous group. Is Wachovia's Crown Classic account for that 76-year-old widow on a fixed income or for that 53-year-old Boomer with two kids in high school and a vacation home, who is expecting a big bonus this year? Obviously it won't meet the needs of both.

Introduction: Meeting the Needs of a Growing Population

When Boomers first started "coming of age" in the late 1960s and early '70s, the focus of marketing in the United States shifted from "adults" to "young adults." Older adults, especially those over 50, were mostly ignored. Then thanks to Richard Nixon's emphasis on the "Silent Majority," some focus on older Americans returned, resulting in the growth of organizations like AARP, once known as the American Association of Retired People.

Founded in 1958 by retired high school principal Dr. Ethel Percy Andrus, AARP started out as the National Retired Teachers Association (NRTA), providing health insurance and other benefits for retired teachers. But then, in the 1960s, due to the enactment of Medicare

Mayer/Freescale Semi :: Mark Mays/Clear Channel :: Mark McAndrew/Torchmark :: Mike McCallister/Humana

and the increased demand from thousands of non-teachers who wanted the same benefits, it was expanded and opened to all Americans 50 and over and became AARP, of which the NRTA is a division.

AARP negotiated discounts on products and services – the majority of which were age-restricted – on behalf of their members, most of whom were retired and on a fixed income. AARP also popularized age "50" as the demarcation from "Adulthood" to "Old Age."

Soon "Senior" discounts grew from a handful of businesses to national and local companies of all shapes and sizes, from the "Early Bird Specials" at the local diner to discounts from drugstore chains granted to anyone over 50, 60 or 65. All seniors qualified because they had reached a certain age and were on a fixed income.

Marketers concluded that everyone over 50 would benefit from products designed for them and quickly introduced age-restricted products and services. Over the next thirty or so years marketers effectively treated everyone over 50 as the same.

Now that half of all Boomers are over 50, and the rest are going to be over 50 by the last day of 2014, it's time to rethink that approach. Marketers need to treat everyone over 50 differently, especially Boomers.

A Brief History of Targeting

Modern marketing and advertising started in the 1850s when J. Walter Thompson began creating newspaper ads. Traditionally, targeting by age has been the easiest and most effective approach and until about 1950, the target for most marketing was simply "Adults."

By the mid-1950s, however, marketers realized they could use TV ads to lure and persuade little Bobby and Susie to ask Mom and Dad to buy products. In the mid-1970s marketers also began to recognize consumers at the older end of the age spectrum. Thus, three distinct age segments were created: Under 18 ("Kids"), 18-49-year-olds ("Adults") and 50+ ("Seniors").

:: David McClanahan/CenterPoint Energy :: Aubrey McClendon/Chesapeake Energy :: Dustan McCoy/Brunswick

Only in the last few years have marketers started to realize 50+ may not be a single group any more. The irony is that Boomers, by their very size, are responsible for creating all the shifts into age segments in marketing over the last 40 years. Almost every time marketers figured out they needed to change the target, to make it more segmented, it was because they had identified an irresistible force that needed their attention: Boomers. Boomers were the young Bobby and Susie of the 1950s. In 1973, the median age of Boomers was 18. By 2004 the median age of Boomers had reached 49. Only since then did marketers realize that the most important demographic wave in history was flowing past the age of 50, creating a new dynamic for the "over 50" segment.

Today, though, three generations are over the age of 50 in America, a total of about 91 million by the end of 2007, according to the U.S. Census. About 45 million (roughly less than half) are Boomers, with another 46 million being members of the G.I. and Silent Generations, those born in 1945 or earlier. Boomers, Silent and G.I. are three distinct "over 50" generations. That's why AARP, the "all things to all people over 50" organization, publishes three editions of every issue of *AARP The Magazine* – one for members in their 50's, another for those in their 60's and still another for members in their 70's and older. Obviously AARP knows something about the "over 50" segment that few marketers understand.

Naturally the rules of targeting Boomers will change as they grow older. Later in this chapter we'll cover more about how to segment Boomers, but the underlying theme of Rule #1 is: *Treat Everyone Differently.*

 **Boom**Box

Words to the Wise

In many companies we meet the "evangelists" who uncover the Boomer opportunity and try to convince management that renewed attention must be paid. Typically, they tell us it is a frustrating experience, even though most executives themselves are over 50.

:: Raymond McDaniel/Moody's :: Mackey McDonald/VF Corporation :: Harold McGraw/McGraw-Hill Companies

One suggestion we make that helps is to change the language. Often the words used to describe the opportunity are "aging consumer" or "aging Boomers." The problem is that emphasizes the wrong word — "aging" and not the word all executives are interested in — "consumers."

Our advice is to sell management on developing programs to reach "consumers at any age" or "today's Boomer consumer." Take "age" out of the discussion, or at least minimize it. There's no pride in being called "aging," and those 50+ execs themselves want to feel relevant and important. Calling them consumers certainly does that.

Boomers Are 78 Million Individuals

When we started the Boomer Project in 2003, we wanted to answer what we called "the second question" of marketers. The first question is, "*Why* target Boomers? Others have addressed that issue: AARP, the media, demographics, and so forth. The second question is, "*How* do we target Boomers?" From the start, we designed our research to answer that question. (The third question, "*How well* are we doing?" won't be answered for a few more years, and our partner, SIR Research, can help via primary marketing research.)

The media has been the most effective communicator of "*Why* target Boomers?" Over the last several years, there have been thousands and thousands of newspaper, magazine, TV and radio features about today's Boomer Consumer, almost all of them using the word "Boomer" in the headline. You can't buy that kind of publicity.

Just look at this list of story topics from a single week in 2005:

- Boomers like muscle cars
- Boomers like new hybrid car/electric cars
- Boomers surf (the Internet) while at work
- Boomers still surf (the ocean)

:: Scott McGregor/Broadcom :: Bill McGuire/UnitedHealth Group :: Scott McNealy/Sun Microsystems :: Jim

- Boomers will be big users of wheelchairs and other mobility devices
- Boomers are flocking to play softball
- Boomers are downsizing, buying condos, running up real estate prices in Hawaii, sparking demand for property in Florida
- Boomers are paying for technology to care for their aging parents
- Boomers are big fans of Goofy

And if anything, the stories have increased. Just google "Boomers" and the hits just keep on coming. However, the good news/bad news is, along with recognizing Boomers as a force in the American economy, there is an impression that "all Boomers are created equal" and they are a homogeneous group.

The truth is, if you put the word "Adults" in place of "Boomers" in the above-mentioned story topics, it would still be accurate. But when you have any population of 78 million (roughly Canada, Australia, Cuba and Chile combined), you're going to have incredible diversity and differences. Yes, *some* Boomers like snow skiing and knitting and French food and shag carpeting and duck hunting and just about anything else you can think of. But not *all* Boomers do.

Reporters and editors need a short-cut to identify who they're talking about, so they just use "Boomers" as a catch-all term for people currently in their 40's and 50's. Ultimately, this is a disservice to marketers who, although they can tap into the shared history and culture of Boomers, must also recognize that they are at various life stages and live a variety of lifestyles. It isn't one size fits all. Ads like the one from Wachovia don't make sense because consumers "over 50" are not all the same.

Some marketers do grasp the diverse nature of today's Boomers. For example, for the last few years Carnival Cruises has been running a TV and print campaign showing the different things one can experience on a cruise, summing up the message with the line "At any one moment there are a million ways to have fun." Carnival understands that Boomers come in all shape and sizes, and doesn't try to force them into a single definition of what to do while on a cruise.

McNerney/Boeing :: Henry Meyer/KeyCorp :: Merrill Miller/National Oilwell Varco :: Stuart Miller/Lennar :: Joe

Another example is a recent ad for tourism in Panama that states, "One beautiful country. Ten inviting destinations." The ad then lists ten distinct areas within Panama, from beaches to rain forests to cities. The marketers understand that a Boomer will look over the list to see what's of interest to them, and will ignore the other, less relevant places.

Articles, news stories and features about "Boomers" may give the mistaken impression of a single, cohesive group of 78 million. They should be segmented like any "Adults" audience – by income, education, values, geography, life stage, and so forth.

Avoid Generalizations

Marketers need to be aware of and sensitive to the media's habit of focusing on the age and life stage of the leading-edge Boomers — the first group, born in 1946 — and applying it to the entire generation. This type of generalization can lead to sweeping marketing decisions that will likely fail to reach the desired target audience.

For example, in January 2006, those 1946 Boomers started celebrating their 60th birthdays. The number of stories about "Boomers turning 60" was overwhelming and over-exaggerated. The fact is that only about three million Boomers turned 60 in 2006, while the other 96% had not. More significantly, more Boomers were born during the second half of the 18-year cohort, according to the U.S. Census. So the actual midpoint of the entire 78 million reaching age *50* — a full ten years younger that that first, smaller batch of Boomers born in 1946 — won't occur until August 2007.

This habit of ascribing attributes of the first Boomers to the entire cohort will likely continue. There will be headlines about "retiring Boomers" although only a small minority will retire at age 62, in 2008. Although the first Boomers are reaching those milestones, even those who are there may be not retiring anytime soon. And the rest of the Boomers aren't even close to retirement. The halfway point of Boomers reaching age 65 is 2022, with the last of the cohort attaining that age on December 31, 2029. That's not exactly imminent.

Moglia/TD Ameritrade Holding :: Surya Mohapatra/Quest Diagnostics :: Larry Montgomery/Kohl's :: Leslie

The truth is that most Boomers are nowhere near retiring. Nor are they about to turn 61, 62 or 63. And understanding today's Boomer Consumer will be a 20-year undertaking.

BoomBox

Who Moved the Bull's-Eye?

A conundrum in marketing today is the continued fascination with the 18-49 age group. Articles in advertising and media trade journals routinely still refer to the "coveted" audience for TV programming as "the 18-49 age segment."

But in a twist on the "chicken and egg" discussion, what came first: Boomers or the "coveted 18-49 segment?"

Want to guess?

That's right, it was Boomers, who began turning 18 in 1964. When half of the cohort reached 18 in 1973, Boomers caught the attention of ABC. Wallowing in third place, the TV conglomerate decided to focus its programming on the huge, young demographic in an attempt to attract viewers.

The top dog in TV at the time was CBS, with its highest-rated shows in 1969 being "Gunsmoke," "Mayberry RFD," "Family Affair," Westerns and family fare. Third-place ABC only had one show in the Top Ten in 1969 – "Marcus Welby, MD." In 1969, the median age of Boomers was 14.

ABC did some research and discovered younger viewers liked half hour comedies and lighter TV fare, so it began revamping its line-up in the early 1970s to draw those millions of Boomer eyeballs to their programs.

Moonves/CBS :: Jackson Moore/Regions Financial :: Pat Moore/Smurfit-Stone :: Charles Moorman/Norfolk

By the mid-1970s, ABC was Number One with shows like "Happy Days," "Laverne & Shirley," "Charlie's Angels" and the "Six Million Dollar Man." ABC had seven out of the Top Ten rated shows in 1976. The median age of Boomers in 1976 was 21.

Here's the rub: The median age of Boomers today is 51. They are quickly aging out of the "coveted" demographic. And ABC, and everyone else, is still more interested in targeting today's 21-year-old than 51-year-old. Yet according to Census Bureau estimates for the U.S. population in 2007, there will be 4,216,048 21-year-olds and even more 51-year-olds, some 4,283,675 strong!

So the target isn't an age segment, it's the demographic segment of Baby Boomers. The same demo it has been for thirty years. They just aren't 18-49 anymore.

Perhaps it's time to shift aim.

Segmenting Today's Boomer Consumer

The cover story of the February 5, 2005 *US News & World Report*, "The Secret Mind: How Your Unconscious Really Shapes Your Decisions," reported that "we are conscious of only about 5 percent of our cognitive activity, so most of our decisions, actions, emotions, and behavior depends on the 95 percent of brain activity that goes beyond our conscious awareness." That means when we ask consumers why they buy, we're really only probing 5% of their conscious mental activity. What they tell us may not be all that meaningful. That is why when it comes to developing a segmentation scheme for today's Boomer Consumer, *actions can speak louder than words*.

Segmenting any audience typically starts with the immutable facts of age and gender. Both are good staring points. Age, as the chart on Page 82 shows, contains two important components — the generational cohort of the consumer (or "Generation"), and their Physical and Cognitive Development.

Southern :: Michael Morris/American Electric :: Daniel Mudd/Fannie Mae :: Anne Mulcahy/Xerox :: James

Generational cohort is important because the time and place in history in which someone matures, or comes of age (ages 15-25) and how the events they experience —political, societal, cultural — affect their worldviews and values. It's what makes Boomers different from their parents and their children.

Physical and Cognitive Development is important because as we age we continue to change and evolve. Boomers in their 40's, 50's and now 60's are different physically and mentally than when they were in their 20's and 30's, as mentioned in Chapter 2. For example, generally Boomer women in their late-40's are at the end or have finished their child-bearing years, although there are some exceptions. By age 50, practically all Boomers have begun experiencing changes in their vision, hearing, mobility, flexibility and other physical attributes. And, according to cognitive psychologists, Boomers in their 50's are becoming less concerned with acquiring material things and more interested in seeking out quality experiences. This "Middle Age" stage of life brings with it the acceptance of the potential reached so far and a more realistic view of what can be achieved in the future.

Age, therefore, provides the foundation of any segmentation scheme. But rather than being an end, it is the start.

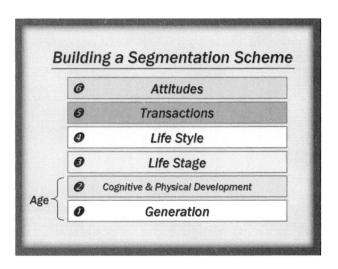

Source: The Boomer Project

The next two levels of a successful segmentation scheme are rooted in choices made by consumers — Life Stage and Life Style. Although consumers today have considerable influence over their Life Stage — married, single, parent, working, retired – some stages are outside of their control. Plus, how one reacts to the Life Stage affects their behavior. For example, consumers can embrace or reject the Life Stages of "Caregiver" or "Grandparent."

Nonetheless, knowing the Boomer Consumer's Life Stage is critically important in determining potential behavior. Do they have kids? How old are the kids? Do they still live at home? Are their parents alive? Where do the parents live and are they in good health? Does the consumer work? Retired? Obviously, each Life Stage comes with its own set of wants and needs.

Similarly, understanding the Life Style and socioeconomic status of the Boomer Consumer is important. Where do they live — in a home, condo, or apartment? What are their interests and activities? Do they have the means to satisfy their wants and needs? Understanding their chosen Life Style reveals much (but not all) about consumer behavior.

In most segmentation schemes, the big "a-ha" comes by overlaying consumer attitudes ("Attitudes") on top of the four stages. But a smarter approach might be to first insert transactional data ("Transactions") into the mix before considering attitudinal differences. As we said earlier, actions speak louder than words.

To obtain transactional information, we work with clients to see who buys what products and services. For segmentation to be of value in the board room, where money is king, it is critically important to understand which customers make you money and which don't.

For example, if analysis of purchase data reveals that 80% of sales come from 20% of customers, guess whose attitudes you'll want to better understand? This 20% customer base could be segmented further to learn more about their attitudes and perceptions. You could then turn your attention to the remaining 80% of current customers to determine how they could be motivated to purchase more, and what constitutes the "model" customer.

The bottom line is the same for any successful segmentation scheme. If you focus on purchase activity — before delving into attitudes — you'll be well on your way to creating a segmentation scheme that will work for your company, organization, and board room.

Summary

The first "new rule" for selling and marketing to today's Boomer Consumer is to treat everyone differently. The old days of grouping everyone "over 50" into a single marketing segment are gone. Similarly, it is a mistake to try to group 78 million consumers into a single segment.

- Marketers today need to rely less on age segments and more on generational segments for the first level of broadest targeting. Age is a consideration, only in that it informs marketers about physical and cognitive stages, as well as life stages (child-bearing years, for example).

- "Over 50" has three distinct generational components – Boomers, Silent and G.I. Their wants and needs differ considerably.

- Don't get fooled by articles and stories about "Boomers." The word "adults" could be just as easily substituted. Any population as large as the Boomer cohort is diverse and has consumers across the full range of every conceivable measurement – socio-economic, income, education, religion, politics, geogra-phy, life style, life stage and more.

- Smart segmentation schemes focus on purchase behavior. Understanding who buys and who doesn't is the best place to start in determining the right segmentation scheme for your business, industry, or organization.

Chapter 6
Rule 2: Use Emotionally Meaningful Concepts, Words and Images

Diane Osborne, 46, had been driving her Chevy Tahoe sport utility vehicle for five years, and was ready to purchase something new. When she first bought the Tahoe, trading it in for a Jeep Cherokee, she took a month to decide, test-driving several different models from various manufacturers.

This time, she thought, would be the same, because she had always been a careful and selective car shopper. But she liked her Tahoe, and now just wanted something similar but higher end: a bit bigger, with more amenities. She thought she'd stay within the GM family because the Tahoe was dependable and relatively maintenance-free. So the first place Diane stopped was the GMC dealership. She bought a Yukon that afternoon and drove it home. She test-drove no other models and shopped no other dealerships.

When asked about it a week later, she said, "It just felt right. It was like my Tahoe, only nicer, and the dealer was nice and easy to work with. I don't know, I just didn't see any reason to prolong the process. I knew what I wanted and there it was."

Diane felt as if she had made a careful, well-thought-out and rational decision. In reality, she had made a gut decision, relying more on emotion and feelings than logic. But Diane is not unusual. As we'll see in this chapter, today's Boomer Consumer buys faster and with more conviction, based more on emotions than thoughts.

Introduction: Buying Decisions Change With Age

For years, marketers understood that consumers make decision three ways – with their heads (rationally), with their hearts (emotionally) and with their guts (instinctively). One rather hidden aspect of this is that the older someone gets, the more likely they are to buy based on gut instinct.

For example, a young adult age 28 may not have a huge income. They find themselves having to make significant purchases to furnish a home or apartment, plan a vacation, or buy a new car. For most big-ticket items, that young adult consumer is going to do thorough research,

O'Brien/Ashland :: Stanley O'Neal/Merrill Lynch :: David O'Reilly/Chevron :: Steve Odland/Office Depot :: Bill comparing and contrasting the features, options and costs to determine the best value. The entire purchase process will be very rational, including post-purchase validation. The younger adult wants to avoid making a mistake they literally cannot afford.

This rational process continues during the life stages of getting married, buying a house, having kids and raising them to their teen years. By the time that younger adult is in their mid-40's or early 50's, they have made something like what seems like 8 billion carefully thought-out purchase decisions. They are also at or nearing their peak earning years, and feel quite experienced in these matters. That collective knowledge built up over the years that now rests soundly in their "gut" (hence the term, "gut instinct").

Boomers are at that stage in their consuming life where most decisions will be based on how they feel, instinctively, about the purchase. The combination of features, benefits and price point of the product or service either does or does not "feel right." Not much time or energy is spent in thinking it through rationally. Sure, Boomers will want the relevant information, but they won't be swayed by "just the facts" into buying the product. They need to be sold emotionally. Hence, *Rule #2: Use emotionally compelling concepts, words and images.*

Reasons to Believe, Not Facts

We set out to learn more about this rule during a national study in 2004. We created two ads targeted to Boomers over 50, promoting the need for retirement planning, for an imaginary firm, BMF Financial.

The ads were directed towards the opposite ends of the rational/emotional spectrum. The first, depicted on page 88, shows a photo of a highway, with the headline "Now that you're 55, the road to retirement has gotten shorter. Make sure you've got the right directions." The copy lays out the facts of what it means to be age 55 and not have a financial plan for your retirement years. The ad promotes a free informational brochure about 55 products for those age 55 and older. The tagline ends with a very rational statement about BMF Financial: "The financial experts."

Osborn/Northern Trust :: Paul Otellini/Intel :: Clarence Otis/Darden Restaurants :: Jim Owens/Caterpillar :: Sam

The ad is the epitome of rational, pinpointing the number 55 and literally showing "the road to retirement." It is as if Joe Friday himself sat down and said "Just the facts, m'am."

The other ad (page 89) takes a much more emotional approach with the headline "Ready to plan for the time of your life?" Along with their photo, it tells the story of Peter and Susan, a 40-something couple, now empty nesters wondering how to prepare for their future. It shares what Mark, their financial planner, had done for them. The tagline is "BMF Financial: Helping you chart your own course."

This ad doesn't even mention the "R" word, retirement, and instead talks only about the future.

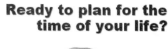

Ready to plan for the time of your life?

Meet Peter and Susan

When the kids moved out and Peter and Susan finally got the house to themselves, it felt differently than they had anticipated. Pretty soon they decided it was a good time to re-evaluate their plans for the future.

Getting a Bearing

Peter called Mark, their financial planner at BMF. Mark spent some time asking questions about their goals, and discovered Peter was going to keep on working in some capacity to well into his late 60's.

Knowing that, Mark, Peter and Susan came up with a plan to re-balance their portfolio for the financial future they envisioned.

That's Why It's Called Planning

At BMF, we realize our clients have unique situations and needs, and that those change frequently. So our planners are prepared to work with you to manage your money in a way that makes it work harder for you.

Spend some time with someone like Mark and you'll see how BMF can help you chart your course. Call us at 1-800-555-1212, or visit us online at bmfonline.com to learn more.

BMF Financial
Helping you chart
your own course

We showed both ads to 1,200 Boomer Consumers ages 42-60. Not surprisingly, the emotional ad was preferred by approximately a three-to-one margin. Consumers told us they could relate more to the second ad, connecting with the people, their story and the feeling the ad presents. Some respondents told us they liked the specific information shared in the first ad, which is missing in the second ad, but they still preferred the emotional version.

Focus on Perspective

In *Ageless Marketing*, David Wolfe writes that companies want to focus on features ("what we're selling") and consumers focus on feelings ("how it makes me feel"). The older consumer, today's Boomer, will respond much faster to messages from their side of the table – from their perspective.

Richard Parsons/Time Warner :: Henry Paulson/Goldman Sachs Group :: George Paz/Express Scripts :: Jeffrey

For instance, Carnival Cruises features a print ad depicting a 40-something couple embracing on the deck of ship, but photographed so close up all you see is their smiling, happy faces and the blue sky and sea behind them. The only thing that's shown of the boat is the railing on which they lean. Rather than a headline, the ad lists the following:

Mike and Sandy Moore.
   Thrill seekers.
      Piano bar regulars.
         Dancing fools.
            Fine dining aficionados.
               Underwater explorers.
                  Sun lovers by days.
                     Star gazers by night.

That's it. Seven *emotionally meaningful reasons* to take a cruise. They don't highlight the features and attributes of the ship. They don't list facts like "Seven restaurants open 24 hours a day," "Telescope for star-watching," "Scuba diving," "Three dance clubs," "Two pools with huge decks." Instead, Carnival gives the reader *reasons* to take a cruise, from the perspective of the consumer.

Advertising experts have spent careers trying to convince clients to talk about emotional end-benefits instead of the physical or functional attributes of a product or service. Norman Berry, former creative director at New York agency Ogilvy & Mather would tell clients that rather than wasting money advertising the features and attributes of their widgets, they should convey the *end benefit* of the widget to consumers. His example was that in one year, Black & Decker sold 250,000 drill bits for their power drills. But that's not what people bought. What people bought was 250,000 holes! Norman knew that nobody buys a drill bit unless they needed a hole. Today's Boomer Consumer wants advertising to deliver reasons to believe, not empty facts.

The Proof Is In the Science

Dr. Laura Carstensen, a professor of psychology and director of the Life-span Institute at Stanford University, found scientific evidence that emotionally compelling messages work better than presenting just straight facts. She conducted research focusing on the social, emotional and cognitive processes that people use to adapt to life circumstances as they age.

In one study she tested consumers of different ages on their ability to recall the emotional components of a story. Younger consumers were better at remembering the facts and rational segments than older consumers. Interestingly, older consumers typically recalled twice as many of the emotional components than the younger ones. Her conclusion, in part, was that older brains value emotional components more and therefore concentrate their recall skills on these segments more than on rational ones.

For a marketer trying to get the attention of an older consumer, like today's Boomer, that means presenting emotionally compelling reasons and not simply lists facts and figures. We'll talk more about Dr. Carstensen's work in the next chapter.

What Works and What Doesn't

Presenting an emotionally compelling message can make the difference between success and failure in an ad campaign. The following ad for Newell motor coaches is typical of what's found in most RV publications. It is a "beauty" shot of the interior and exterior of the vehicle, and the copy includes specific facts like "the impressive 625 horsepower Caterpillar C-15 engine with ZF AS-Tronic transmission [that] produces 2,050 lb-ft of torque."

While the photography is elegant and the motor home has a unique front grill, Norman Berry of Ogilvy would say this ad is all about drill bits, instead of holes. Only in this case, the drill bits cost about $400,000.

The second ad, for Tiffin Motor Homes, isn't about the motor home at all, but what it does for the owner. The line between the top and bottom photos is "From an empty house to my granddaughter's first laugh." The tag line is simply "How far will your Tiffin take you?"

Although a print ad in a magazine isn't going to close the sale on these $400,000 rolling estates, it is vital in initially attracting customers. The purchase cycle for these investments is long and protracted, especially considering that the loans involve legal and financial processes similar to buying a regular home or condo.

Yet the vast majority of the ads in most RV oriented magazines are about the features and attributes of each manufacturer's product. However, Tiffin seems to grasp the concept that their audience, the older consumer judging by the casting, will respond to an emotionally meaningful message and will feel that Tiffin understands them at this stage of life.

SIR Research, the marketing research partner of the Boomer Project, worked closely with the trade association for the recreational vehicle industry, *GO RVing*, on their advertising campaign. In the last 10 years, SIR has done several studies to help *GO RVing* better understand the underlying motivations for RV vacations. The Go RVing Coalition's advertising agency, the Richards Group, has developed a print and TV campaign celebrating all the things that make an RV vacation unique and memorable. The theme of the emotionally compelling stories is, "What will you discover?" All of the ads are about the experience delivered by an RV vacation or trip.

It makes sense for advertisers to use emotionally compelling concepts, words and images with Boomers, who are now in a cognitive and psychological stage of being less interested in acquiring material things and more interested in acquiring better life experiences. You still need to provide relevant information to make it easier for the consumer to learn about your product or service, as you'll see in the next chapter. But you also have to craft it in emotional terms.

This doesn't mean your marketing communications have to be sappy or overly "warm and fuzzy." Your message can be funny and endearing. For example, Universal Studios advertises their theme park in Orlando by showing scenes of people enjoying different aspects of the park, with a twist. In one commercial, a woman relaxes poolside as her voice narrates that she wants "to be pampered by natives." The camera pulls back to show a costumed character of Frankenstein painting her toenails. Another scene depicts a woman on a thrill ride sitting between her two children. Her voice-over narrates that she wants "to get closer to my kids." As they then turn a corner and everyone gets scared, she pulls both kids into her lap as only a mother would do.

Gary Rainwater/Ameren :: David Ratcliffe/Southern Co :: Dennis Reilley/Praxair :: Steve Reinemund/PepsiCo ::

It's a funny commercial that provides emotionally compelling reasons to visit Universal Orlando without a laundry list of costumed characters or scary rides. But, no matter what your message, it needs to be positive, as we'll discuss in the next chapter.

Summary

Today's Boomer Consumers are at the age and cognitive and psychological stage where they will buy faster and with more conviction based on instinct and emotions and how they "feel" about a product or service. Therefore, to get their attention and be persuasive marketers must use emotionally meaningful concepts, words and images.

These emotions can be presented as "reasons" to think, feel or act differently about your product or service. They don't have to be sappy or overly "warm and fuzzy," but can be funny and endearing.

Research shows that older consumers recall emotional narrative in stories more so than rational facts. This provides an opening for marketers to think about how they can recast their facts into compelling reasons to believe. Boomer Consumers especially are buying drill bits not to own the actual equipment, but to make holes. Effective marketing reflects an understanding of that concept.

Glenn Renwick/Progressive :: Tom Renyi/Bank of New York :: Dowd Ritter/AmSouth Bancorp :: Brian Roberts/

Chapter 7
Rule 3: Be Positive

*S*haron Johnson, 60, has been a movie buff all her life. During her teen years, back in the late 1950s and early '60s, she became enamored with the horror movie genre. Films such as Vincent Price's "The Fly" and "The Raven" and Hitchcock's "Psycho" and "The Birds" provided her a spine-tingling feeling and adrenaline rush she really enjoyed. This continued through the 1980s, when the genre was dominated by "The Exorcist," "The Omen," "Halloween," and "Carrie."

Yet despite her lifelong love of a good scare, Sharon hasn't seen a horror movie on TV or at the theatre in over ten years. They simply don't interest her anymore. Why? She'll tell you that she doesn't like them. They are to negative she says.

Sharon is typical of Boomers her age. They don't respond to negative concepts, words, and images. They prefer the positive.

Introduction: Emphasize the Positive

So far we've discussed treating today's Boomer Consumer differently – they are far from all the same. We've also learned the importance of using emotionally compelling concepts, words, and images. Another important rule is being positive in how and what we say to today's Boomer Consumer. Using negativity will result in the risk of having them ignore us, just like Sharon Johnson now disregards horror movies.

Back when Matt was a new account executive at New York-based Ogilvy & Mather Advertising, he learned much about the advertising business, including the three tasks of any effective ad. They are, in sequence:

1. Get somebody's attention.
2. Communicate something.
3. Persuade the viewer or reader to think, feel, or act differently.

If the first rule is to get their attention, then it is very important to understand what today's Boomers pay attention to, and what they ignore. They ignore negative messages.

Rohr/PNC Financial Services :: Kevin Rollins/Dell :: Matthew Rose/Burlington Santa Fe :: Paula Reynolds/Safeco

The Cognitive Processes of Positive Thinking

As mentioned in Chapter 6, the research of Dr. Laura Carstensen, professor of psychology and director of the Life-span Institute at Stanford University, focuses on the social, emotional, and cognitive processes that people use to adapt to life circumstances as they age. She concentrates specifically on motivation and emotional functioning, studying the ways in which people process emotional images, concepts, and words. One of her significant findings, written up in peer-reviewed academic journals, is that the older a consumer gets, the less likely they'll respond to neutral or negative images, concepts, or words. So if you aren't positive in your message or "materials," older consumers will not respond to your efforts. You'll fail to get their attention.

Dr. Carstensen did a series of tests with consumers grouped into three age brackets – "young" (under 35), "middle" (35-54), and "old" (55+). In one test she showed consumers photos that were positive, neutral, and negative. The positive pictures included images like two cute bunny rabbits, and a husband embracing his wife and child. The neutral photos were of inanimate objects like filing cabinets and soup bowls. The negative photos were stark images of a bird stuck in an oil spill, and a cockroach walking on someone's dinner plate. She showed the same series of 10+ images to all the respondents then asked them to recall the various images they had seen.

At first, the scores were as expected. Across all three image types, positive, neutral and negative, the average number of images recalled by "young" and "middle" aged participants was higher than that of "old" participants. Dr. Carstensen had figured this would likely happen, knowing that older consumers would have more difficulty in recalling images. Short-term memory is clinically shown to decline as one ages.

But what surprised Dr. Carstensen was how older participants seemed to do a much better job of recalling the positive images versus the negative and neutral images. The "young" participants recalled on average 3.7 positive images, "middle" aged respondents recalled 4.0 images and "old" recalled 3.1, which is not all that great of a difference.

:: Bob Rossiter/Lear :: Michael Roth/Interpublic Group :: John Rowe/Exelon :: Pat Russo/Lucent Technologies ::

When it came to recalling the negative images, however, Dr. Carstensen found that the average number of negative images recalled by "young" participants was 3.7 (the same as the positive images). "Middle" aged respondents recalled 3.6, slightly less than they had remembered of the positive images. But "old" respondents only recalled 1.7 negative images, or half as many as the younger participants, and, fascinatingly, about half of the number of positive images they remembered! The neutral scores had a similar pattern: 2.5 for "young," 2.7 for "middle" and only 0.7 for "old." This study suggested that older consumers are processing negative and neutral images differently than younger consumers, at least in terms of recall.

In another test, Dr. Carstensen asked subjects to choose between two different models of cars. Older adults spent more time reviewing their positive features, whereas younger adults were likely to focus equally on both positive and negative aspects. Dr. Carstensen concluded that, as one ages, a developmental pattern emerges: the willingness to process negative images, concepts, and words ("material") in youth decreases as people get older. She calls this the "*positivity effect.*" Younger minds have an increased memory for and attention to negative information, while older minds have an increased memory for and attention to the positive.

Dr. Carstensen and her colleagues went one step further by conducting neuroanatomical imaging studies. They connected people to MRI machines to watch activity within the portion of the brain called the *amygdala*, a key center for emotion processing. She watched to see if the amygdala would "activate" and essentially send along images seen by the eyes to the upper temporal lobes for further processing. What she found was that the amygdala responds differently to positive and negative information with age. Both older and younger adults show similar amygdala activity when viewing positive pictures, but older adults show less activity compared to their younger peers when viewing negative images.

Dr. Carstensen's work suggests that older adults have subconsciously and literally trained their brains to ignore negative material. So if you are marketing to today's older Boomer Consumer, it's essential to be positive. Otherwise the consumer will simply not even see or respond to your message.

Carstensen hopes that her findings will be used to improve the lives of older adults beyond better marketing and advertising. If older people remember positive information better than negative, she writes in academic journals, it would be wise to restructure health messages in a more positive light, for example. Even subtle changes such as emphasizing the benefits of exercise and healthy diet rather than the consequences of failure to engage in these activities could be powerful.

Whether or not it's a direct result of Dr. Carstensen's work, already various aging and health organizations have recast their messages to older Americans. Instead of promoting "exercise," some are now telling older adults to "stay active" (not that the term "exercise" is a negative, but it doesn't seem to be working either). The Active Aging Partnership (www.agingblueprint.org), for example, advises agency organizations to emphasize "physical activity" for 30 minutes a day instead of exercise, because they believe it will motivate more people. An initiative in Texas, Active for Life (www.activeforlife.info) is doing the same thing.

Don't Look! It's a Pink Elephant

The scientific proof that older minds literally don't process negative concepts, words, and images should have a big impact on anyone trying to market to today's Boomer Consumer. In an ideal world, this would mean that negative advertising and marketing messages aimed at older consumers would disappear. No more headlines like, "I wish I had known" in an ad about the risks of macular degeneration. All messages would be stated in the positive.

But, alas, many marketers are unaware of how brains at any age process negative concepts, words, and images. In truth, brains must learn to process the positive aspect of the stimuli in order to then process the negative aspect. It may happen in nanoseconds, but it happens. For example, right now we want you to <u>not</u> think of a pink elephant. <u>Don't</u>

picture a pink elephant in your head. <u>Don't</u> close your eyes and see that plump, trunk-swaying, pink-colored creature dancing about in your mind's eye. Just <u>don't</u> do it.

A ha! You did it anyway. At least at first, but then you probably put the mental equivalent of the universal "Do Not" red slash symbol over top of the image. That's how the brain processes most negatives, by thinking of the positive first and then the negative.

As you age, your brain loses some of its processing speed and naturally starts to sort the information coming in from all five of the senses. The brain does a type of triage, prioritizing the input to more efficiently send it along for further processing (basically what Dr. Carstensen calls "amygdala activation"). When faced with negative input, like this headline: "Don't Miss This Weekend's Sale," the first processing of that message is "<u>Do</u> Miss This Weekend's Sale." Then, nanoseconds later, the brain processes the negative.

Knowing this, why don't advertisers and marketers, clamoring to get your attention, stop using negatives across the board and use positive phrasing instead? In the example, the positive phrasing could be something like "Come to This Weekend's Sale." If you still want some urgency, add "Or You'll Miss Out."

This subconscious two-step processing of negative concepts, words, and images applies to all communications. For instance, Matt's two-year-old daughter, Mia, is learning language. When he tells her, "<u>Don't</u> put that marble in your mouth" she immediately does exactly that, whether she'd previously considered it or not. When he tells her "Keep that marble in your hand, hold it tight," she keeps it away from her mouth. At least for a while, then, like everything else in her hands, she puts it near the mouth. But the mere suggestion – even if it's phrased in a negative – results in her doing exactly what he tells her <u>not</u> to do. That's how she learns to process language that includes a negative.

Think of your own behavior in business communications. Do you end letters or emails with "Don't hesitate to call if you have questions?"

What is the likely response? The reader will hesitate to call. If you sign off with "Please call with any questions," you'll more likely get calls.

This becomes especially true with today's older Boomer Consumers. They not interested in doing two-step processing to get your message. By being positive, you greatly improve your chances of getting their attention, the first rule in advertising and marketing.

The New Language of Aging

Another aspect of language and being positive is the need to use terms and expressions that today's Boomer Consumer responds to and feels is appropriate. The most important term is the one you use to identify them. Should you call them "seniors," "Boomers," or what?

In American business and European society, to be seen as a "senior" is to be at the top of the class. It's a rank of privilege and respect: "Senior Vice-President," "Senior Advisor," even "college senior."

But such is not the case in modern American society. Over the last 40 years, the term "Senior Citizen" has developed strong negative connotations. This is due at least in part to the frequent portrayal by the entertainment and advertising industries of senior citizens as feeble, weak, poor, confused, and just plain goofy (remember the movie "Grumpy Old Men" and Wendy's "Where's the Beef"?).

Because of this, in recent years, marketers have been careful about using the actual word "senior." They have developed a long list of transparent euphemisms: "mature adults," "active adults," "golden years," "third agers," or tagging items for older adults with the word "silver" or "mature."

Although these substitutes may carry less negative baggage, when it comes to Boomers, none are acceptable. A national study conducted by the Boomer Project in 2003 found that not a single one these terms was appropriate — not "senior," "active adult," or anything similar. Recently the media has embraced the word "Boomer" to describe everyone born between 1946-64, and we think that label will stick.

Circuit City Stores :: John Schuessler/Wendy's International :: Jeffrey Schwartz/ProLogis :: Lee Scott/Wal-Mart

Based on our research, we know that marketers who want to describe Boomers should avoid expressions that refer to age or getting old. Instead, the terms need to address continuing development and should be forward-looking. Boomers are a long way from finished. So far we haven't seen any names that really fit the bill. As you've seen in this book, our own approach is to refer to Boomers as "today's Boomer Consumer." Sometimes we'll refer to them as older Boomers, used like one would use "older brother" or "older sister," more as a statement of fact and not a description of an age or condition ("aging").

As discussed earlier in the book, we recommend that marketers avoid using "aging Boomers" or "aging consumers." Those expressions put the emphasis on the wrong part, the "aging," and not on the part that matters in business, "consumers." Moreover, the decision-makers at the very top in most organizations today are themselves older Boomers. Do they want the "aging" label attached to them? No way.

When it comes to a term of respect for older Boomers, we won't know what phrases will work until Boomers themselves decide, probably not until after 2011, when the first ones reach 65. Don't be surprised if they circle back and decide they'd like to be called "senior" after all, with emphasis on the positive connotations, of course. By then, it may not be such a rank "rank."

Other terms related to "aging" that may go out of fashion include "retirement." Many Boomers won't ever fully "retire," especially as dictionary.com defines it:

Re-tire, **noun:**

1. To withdraw, or go away or apart, to a place of privacy, shelter, or seclusion: *He retired to his study.*

2. To go to bed: *He retired at midnight.*

3. To withdraw from office, business, or active life, usually because of age: *to retire at the age of sixty.*

4. To fall back or retreat in an orderly fashion and according to plan, as from battle, an untenable position, danger, etc.

5. To withdraw or remove oneself: *After announcing the guests, the butler retired.*

Boomers will create a new stage where they no longer work at a job to earn a living but are instead doing work they love to enjoy life and stay vital. The term "retirement" will fall out of use and ultimately disappear in a generation or two, gone the way of the buggy whip or the manual typewriter.

Other changes for traditional terms typically associated with aging and older adults are also on the horizon. If a term like "handicapped" can be replaced with "disabled," and "global warming" can be changed to "climate change," "nursing home" might well be replaced with "life care community" and "assisted living" with "community with services."

Terms like "aging," even prefaced with "healthy" or "successful" may ultimately disappear because they focus on a negative process that involves decline, decay, fading, wearing out, and wasting away. The shift may be towards positive developments associated with growing older and maturing, with terms such as advancing, progressing, ripening, evolving, extending, and even just plain "growing older." "Growing older" doesn't come with the same negative connotation often associated with "aging." It is simply a statement of fact. Children grow older, as do teenagers. Why can't adults?

An Example of Positive Positioning

Some advertisers are catching on. The expression, "Beauty is more than skin deep" aptly describes Dove's recent "Pro-Age" effort as part of their "Campaign for Real Beauty." The ads, which feature tastefully posed, completely naked women over 50, shot by famed photographer Annie Leibowitz, began appearing in women's magazines like *Ladies Home Journal* in March 2007. Like the "Calendar Girls," older women in the British movie of that title who also posed nude, they immediately caused a stir. Reporters, journalists, and bloggers commented on the power, impact, and appropriateness of showing such women on TV and in print and for, of all things, beauty products. In fact, the Federal Communications Commission (FCC) even ruled that TV commercials featuring nude women couldn't run on U.S. TV. The ruling was based on the fact that the women are obviously nude, even though tastefully displayed. Completely nude people are not allowed in advertising on public airways.

Despite this setback, the Dove campaign works for two reasons. It follows the first rule of advertising — get the audience's attention. Dove has certainly done that by using attractive naked older models.

Secondly, it avoids the negative. Even without the naked older women, the underlying strategy and brand name accent the positive; "Pro-Age" is not "anti-aging." It effectively re-positions every other player in the "anti-aging" market as lacking in understanding of today's older female consumer. By turning the category upside down and taking ownership of the term, Dove has pre-empted anyone else coming out with "Pro-Age." Others who do so will only strengthen Dove's hold on the position.

Dove's overall approach of recasting and redefining beauty in terms most consumers understand and embrace is also an example of "Blue Ocean" strategy, as described in the book *Blue Ocean Strategy* by W. Chan Kim and Renée Mauborgneand. Rather than doing bloody battle with competitors in one part of the ocean, companies should venture out into the blue, open water where they can make their competitors obsolete. Dove has done that, leaving behind the other cosmetic, health, and beauty products battling over an idealized view of superficial, youthful beauty. Their "Campaign for Real Beauty" and "Pro-Age" efforts leave everyone else behind in the "Red Ocean."

Surprisingly, so far most other players in the health and beauty industry don't seem to be worried about Dove's zig to their zag, but consumers appear to be buying it— literally. The bulletin boards of

Utilities :: Jay Sidhu/Sovereign Bancorp :: Harris Simmons/Zions Bancorp :: David Simon/Simon Property Group

www.campaignforrealbeauty.com are filled with hundreds of supportive comments from frustrated consumers, who are sick of rail-thin models with perfect features.

The www.doveproage.com Web site also shows a video from the consumer research on the "Pro-Age" TV spot. Along with positive feedback, the video also includes comments from women who are offended by the nudity and don't think American women would approve. But the longer the video plays, the more the viewer begins to realize that the naysayers have missed the point about breaking down stereotypes. Ultimately, of course, consumers will vote on Dove Pro-Age with their money, which is what matters to marketers and executives. Nevertheless, Dove's marketing campaign shows a "positive" understanding of today's Boomer Consumer.

Summary

When it comes to structuring your messages to reach today's Boomer Consumer, make sure it is positive.

- Boomer Consumers are entering a stage of life when their brains begin to literally ignore negative concepts, words, and images, according to research by Dr. Laura Carstensen, a Stanford University professor.

- The brain processes negatives in two steps; first, thinking the positive and then applying the negative to it. This is another reason to structure your selling and marketing messages in the positive.

- The language of aging and the terms used to describe it will change and evolve as Boomers grow older. So stay away from traditional terms associated with previous generations of older consumers. Boomers won't respond to them.

Chapter 8
Rule 4: Realize More Information is Better

avid Blankenship, 53, has been a professional photographer for 30 years. His photos have been used in magazine and newspaper ads, annual reports, corporate brochures, and on Web sites. He is extremely talented and very tuned into the world of advertising and marketing.

At a recent dinner party with contemporaries, the discussion turned to an advertising campaign for a new Lexus that can parallel park itself. Everyone agreed that the idea was very cool but still hard to believe. The conversation then turned to car advertising in general.

"Why are so many just scenes of the car driving down winding roads, with practically no information provided at all?" David wondered aloud. "At least with the Lexus commercial, I know what it is they are trying to tell me about the car. Most of the others don't say much of anything."

The comments turned to other consumer items - trucks, soft drinks, beers, insurance products and more – with the point being that nothing had a point! Like David, the dinner guests were well-educated professionals in their late 40's and 50's, and they all agreed that most commercials were about nothing much at all.

Most Boomers think advertising provides very little relevant information, or doesn't even give them "just the facts" to make an informed decision. Whose fault is that, the Boomers or the advertisers?

Introduction: Grading Advertisers and Advertising

In 2004 the Boomer Project fielded a national study among Boomers and younger adults. One purpose was to see if Boomers indeed felt that advertisers were no longer targeting messages to them. Our ongoing assumption was that Boomers, especially those already over 50 and therefore outside the traditional target market of 18-49, would tell us they think most advertising is aiming too young or too old.

land/Northwest Airlines :: David Steiner/Waste Management :: Robert Stevens/Lockheed Martin :: Ron Sugar/

One series of questions we posed to over 1,400 consumers was about advertising in general. First we asked consumers about a list of attributes often associated with advertising:

- Get my attention
- Give me information I need
- Make it easy for me to get more information
- Increase my interest in the product or service
- Understand my needs
- Be enjoyable
- Be believable
- Be easy to follow or read
- Show people and lifestyles I can relate to
- Target people my age
- Target people younger than me

We asked consumers how important each dimension was to them personally; they responded on a five-point scale from "Very Important" to "Very Unimportant." Then we asked them to grade each dimension using a system of A, B, C and so forth. This technique enabled us to assess the gap between what people tell us is important and the advertising industry's ability to deliver on that dimension. Because we later asked the respondents their year of birth, we could sort and analyze the results by age and generation.

Show Me the Info

What we found was consistent with our assumptions. First, Boomers over 50 told us that the most important attributes were the basics: "Give me information I need" (91% said "Very Important" or "Somewhat Important"), "Make it easy for me to get more information" (91%), and "Be believable" (91%) topped the list. In fact, every attribute was rated by the majority of Boomers over 50 as "Very/Somewhat Important"

Northrop Grumman :: Jay Sugarman/IStar Financial :: Martin Sullivan/American International Group :: John

except for one. "Targets people younger than me" only garnered a score of 19%. Not surprisingly, Boomers over 50 regarded that particular aspect of advertising as unimportant.

What follows is the percentage of respondents who answered "Very/ Somewhat Important" for these attributes:

Get my attention	84%
Give me information I need	*91%*
Make it easy for me to get more information	*91%*
Increase my interest in the product or service	84%
Understand my needs	82%
Be enjoyable	85%
Be believable	*91%*
Is easy to follow or read	87%
Shows people and lifestyles I can relate to	73%
Targets people my age	73%
Targets people younger than me	*19%*

These "importance" scores are consistent with what the younger adults, ages 18-40, also told us about advertising in the study.

But knowing what is important only tells half of the story. When Boomers graded advertisers on their ability to deliver on each of these dimensions, what we learned startled us.

Boomers, especially those over 50, give advertising a very low grade overall and the gaps between "Importance" and delivery are significant:

Dimension	Percent Grading "A" or "B"	Percent Very/Some-what Important	Gap
Get my attention	42%	84%	-42
Give me information that I need	29%	91%	-62
Make it easy for me to get more information	37%	91%	-54
Increase my interest in the product or service	26%	84%	-58
Understand my needs	19%	82%	-63
Be enjoyable	38%	85%	-47
Be believable	17%	91%	-74
Is easy to follow or read	49%	87%	-38
Shows people and lifestyles I can relate to	24%	73%	-49
Targets people my age	24%	73%	-49
Targets people younger than me	71%	19%	+52

Across all dimensions save one, less than half of Boomers over 50 graded advertising with an "A" or "B." The only dimension earning a top grade was, "Targets people younger than me," in which 71% of Boomers over 50 graded advertisers with an "A" or "B."

The grade point average across all other dimensions was a "D+"! More significantly, the gaps between what Boomers over 50 told us was important for advertisers to accomplish and how they delivered were huge. Overwhelming, even.

Nine out of 10 Boomers told us they want advertising to "be believable" and not even 2 out of 10 graded advertisers as doing a good job at it. Only 3 out of 10 stated that advertisers were doing a good job at giving them the information they needed and not even 4 out of 10 said they made it easy to get more information.

Based on these scores, the advertising industry needs to take a good, hard look as to how it delivers information. How long would a retailer stay in business if it failed to meet its customers' needs? If Wal-Mart customers said "good value for the money" was a top attribute and Wal-Mart raised its prices above those of competitors, they probably wouldn't be around long. We think it is time marketers and advertisers address the problem and communicate better with Boomers, before they lose them forever.

Young adults in our study also gave advertisers poor grades. But their overall grades were 25% higher across the board than the grades awarded by Boomers. Their average was, in fact, a middle "C." Also 51% of younger adults said advertisers deserve an "A" or "B" for "targeting people my age," compared to only 24% of Boomers over 50.

A 2006 survey done by TV Land, a cable network popular among Boomers that reruns classic TV shows, found that half of Boomers paid minimal attention to ads targeting young adults; a third are actually less likely to buy the advertised product. This further illustrates the serious gap between what Boomer Consumers want and what advertisers are actually delivering.

That's Entertainment!

Obviously there is tremendous room for improvement in trying to connect with today's Boomer Consumer. This is especially true in looking at the most important things Boomers want from advertisers – "Give me the information I need," "Make it easier for me to get more information," and "Be believable." In all three instances, delivery of those attributes is poor. A cause may be the mindset of most marketers

Termeer/Genzyme :: Kent Thiry/DaVita :: Kennedy Thompson/Wachovia :: John Thompson/Symantec :: Garrett

and their advertising agencies – the common belief being that no one likes advertising so we have to entertain first and inform second.

Nowhere is that mindset more apparent than in the largest advertising showcase of the year, the Super Bowl. Its ads can reach an estimated 90 million viewers, possibly more when you consider the hype they engender as well as the Internet downloads by folks who don't even watch football! Marketers spent upwards of $2.3 million for 30 seconds of advertising time for the 2007 Super Bowl, and the vast majority simply tried to entertain the viewing audience. Precious few attempted to communicate anything.

Of course, the Super Bowl is more entertainment than sport, and over the years the ads have become nearly as significant as the game. But that doesn't explain why marketers and advertisers think that *all* advertising must be entertaining, first and foremost, in the hopes that people will "like them" and buy their product. Somehow they've lost sight of an equally important factor: Providing actual information to the consumer.

That "entertainment" mindset may not work with most other advertising. Trade magazines, for example, are read by consumers who are collecting information and knowledge related to their job or profession rather than entertainment. That's a perfect opportunity for an ad to deliver actual information.

TV news programs and newspapers offer additional opportunities for information that's more than entertainment. In 2005, the Newspaper Association of America conducted a consumer study on media and advertising. Readers said that rather than being a distraction, advertisements were a destination – a reason why they read the paper. This is in contrast to TV, radio, and magazines in which ads were mostly seen as distractions. Even so, the survey found some newspaper ads still didn't contain enough information necessary for the consumer to make a decision. This includes obvious and important "details," such as the business's location, hours of operation, and phone number.

More Is Better

A related problem is the myth that consumers don't or won't read much text in an ad. In advertising, the text is called "body copy" and the current belief is that consumers have short attention spans so you should keep it to a minimum. But the opposite is true: More is better.

Back in the early 1980s the trade group for advertisers, the American Association of Advertising Agencies (AAAA), ran an ad in major magazines to make a case for advertising. The ad showed a photo of the latest and most sophisticated home stereo component equipment at the time — receivers, tape decks, turntables, and speakers. The headline was "Why are most stereo ads stupid, except when you're in the market for a stereo?" The copy went on to explain that only consumers interested in a particular product or service, that is, your best prospects, will pay attention to your ad. The underlying message was it is important to provide them with information they need and make it easy for them to get more information.

Providing that information in ads and other marketing materials requires more words, not fewer. In the direct mail business, historically the mail packages with more component parts and longer copy generate better response rates than the ones with shorter copy. According to *Direct Marketing Rules of Thumb* by Nat Bodian, four-page letters pull twice the response as two-page versions. An interested prospect wants as much information as possible to help them make a decision. A disinterested consumer throws away the direct mail piece regardless of the length.

Why don't more advertisers apply that logic to their advertising? We don't know. All we do know is that consumers, especially Boomer Consumers, tell us they want more information and the advertisers fail to deliver.

 # **Boom**Box

Getting It Right

The Vanguard Group, which sells mutual funds and other investment products, has been running ads in the business section of major newspapers that present the message using an easy-to-understand metaphor of a chapter from a book. "Chapter 15 — Lifetime Income" is the header of the ad. The chapter title: "How to reach retirement and actually get to stay there," successfully draws the reader further into the ad without making too boastful a claim or over-promising anything.

The ad also contains plenty of copy explaining their offerings. Far too often advertisers fear older consumers don't want "too much information" in an ad. While long, boring, uninteresting ads can certainly work against you, our research indicates a frustration among Boomers because advertisers tell them too little. To take action and make a purchasing decision, the reader needs to know something worth acting upon. This ad delivers.

Additionally the ad acknowledges Vanguard's role in the consumer's life. They aren't the one and only answer, just there to help. The ad doesn't boast that Vanguard has all the answers, just some related to properly funding the retirement you want. So even if you're in a rocking chair, you can still rock on.

John Tyson/Tyson Foods :: Mike Ullman/JC Penney :: Daniel Ustian/Navistar International :: Roy Vallee/Avnet ::

"Missing the Boat" Online

Recently a large financial services firm admitted in the headline of its magazine ad that the insurance and investing business is so complicated they were dedicating themselves to making it easier to understand. Sounds great, doesn't it? The short body copy explained the company's commitment to helping make these topics less complicated and enabling you to make the right choices. The ad ends with "Because when it comes to planning for your future and that of your family, being well-informed is always the smartest path."

That's it. No actual information is provided about how or what the company is doing to make it easy. Just that they think "being well-informed is ... the smartest path." They don't provide that information, but want you to like them because they know you'll need information. This is a classic example of an advertiser creating a message to get your attention and then essentially dropping the ball by failing to actually communicate anything.

Sadly, consumers have gotten used to advertising short-changing them in delivering useful information. Advertisers have effectively taught consumers to ignore most ads because they don't contain anything of value, except perhaps the Web site address. Because that's where the consumer is more likely to actually get information. Boomers are just like young adults in this capacity; they routinely search for product and service information online because it isn't readily available anywhere else. In a recent study by the Pew Internet & American Life Project, 80% of Boomers search for product information online, as do 80% of young adults.

Like many advertisers, the "less complicated" financial services company did provide the Web address. So we went to the site, and found...nothing. No reference to making anything easier or less complicated. Instead the Web site contained only information about the company, and nothing about how to understand the complicated industry. And ironically, the current ad wasn't even referenced on the site! Instead it featured the TV branding campaign, which contains even *less* information.

You can probably think of several instances where you've run across this problem online. You've seen an ad on TV or in print for a particular product or service, making some claim that gets your attention. You go online to find out more about the claim, and you find...nothing. It's sad but true: most marketers don't connect the dots between what the advertising department is promoting and what's on the Web site.

Think about your own organization's marketing efforts. Are your off-line messages connected to your online messages, and vice versa? If not, you might want to think about remedying the situation. Boomers will go online in search of more information and will quickly click to another site if the search is overly cumbersome or difficult. Google makes it easy for them to find competitors. You can avoid this predicament altogether by putting your information in your ads. Barring that, make sure it's on your company Web site and easy to find.

Information Isn't Facts

Even though today's Boomers are seeking information from marketers, that doesn't mean they only want bare facts and figures, as discussed in Chapter 6. Your message needs to contain emotionally compelling "reasons to believe."

You as a marketer need to convince them in a meaningful way that your product or service is relevant, believable, and unique. If you can provide specialized and compelling reasons to believe, you're well on your way to winning them over. If you have nothing unique to say, at least communicate your message in a distinguished fashion, or with a distinctive attitude. For example, Southwest flies from point to point just like any other airline, but their attitude and approach is unlike any other. They make it fun, even in how they deliver the standard "...and stow your tray tables in their upright and locked position" spiel required by the FAA. It comes through in the advertising as well, which often shows people in awkward situations while the announcer says "Need to get away? Southwest offers low fares to places across the country."

The "Cave Man" and "Gecko" campaigns for GEICO insurance are other examples. In fact, there's talk of the GEICO "Cave Man" getting his own TV show! GEICO is selling insurance that is virtually identical to insurance sold by everyone else, but they go about it in a distinctive manner. So if you don't have anything new or different to say, at least say it in a unique way.

Also remember that Boomers have been consuming advertising since they were five years old, sitting in front of that black-and-white TV back in the 1950s and 60s. Boomers are the most experienced mass media consumers in the history of humankind (so far). They've seen just about every advertising trick. They are jaded and still time-crunched. That means your messages need to be honest and direct, served up in easy-to-digest chunks that get to the point. The last thing you want is the Boomer to see your message, scratch their head, and go "Huh?" just like David Blankenship's dinner guests. They won't bother to figure it out if it is too difficult or obtuse. A message such as the financial services ad pledging to make it less complicated but then not doing anything about it is likely lost on today's Boomer.

You don't have to spoon-feed Boomers, either. Because they've seen it all already, you'll want to treat them as if they're at least as smart as you. They'll quickly add up what you're communicating and complete the thought, if it's served up in an interesting, compelling, and relevant fashion.

Succeeding in developing effective advertising for today's Boomer Consumer is hard work. If it were easy, the airways and print media would be overflowing with great ads. But it can be less difficult if you remember that Boomers want more information, not less.

Summary

Marketers and advertisers need to deliver relevant, detailed advertising that connects with today's Boomer Consumer.

- Boomers want advertising that gives them information they need, makes it easy to get more information, and is believable. However, Boomers believe marketers and advertisers are failing to do this.

Tom Watjen/UnumProvident :: Wendell Weeks/Corning :: David Weidman/Celanese :: Bill Weldon/Johnson &

- Boomers feel most advertising is targeting younger people, and depicting people and lifestyles unrelated to them. As a result, they are less interested in the product or service advertised.

- Make sure your advertising contains enough relevant, emotionally compelling information. Remember that more, rather than less copy is always better for your best prospects.

- If the information isn't in your ad or marketing materials, make sure it is easy to find on your Web site. Boomers will seek out product information online and want the process to be easy and the messages consistent with what they've seen or heard via traditional media.

Chapter 9
Rule 5: Tell a Story

B rad Lynch, 50, has been in healthcare marketing for most of his career. For the first half he held jobs in corporate and product marketing at large technology companies. During the second half he's been servicing those very companies as a marketing services firm, specializing in pubic relations and producing corporate communications materials like brochures and annual reports.

Brad is such an expert on how to effectively use public relations to help market healthcare technology that he is often asked to lead seminars and give speeches at annual conventions and meetings. When he does those events, he rarely if ever practices beforehand and talks without slides or notes.

Every event that collects evaluations of the speaker or presenter reports that Brad has the best scores anyone can get. Never does he disappoint his audience.

What's the secret of his success?

He tells stories. Depending on how long he is asked to speak, he'll tell from three to seven stories, each illustrating a point about how to use PR effectively. When asked how he came to develop this technique, Brad says, "It's easier for me. I only have to remember three to seven things – the story titles, if you will – and the rest naturally falls from there. Since I actually experienced each story, there's nothing to remember or practice."

It appears Brad has figured something out that great communicators have known for centuries. Stories are the most effective way to communicate ideas and concepts. This is also true in advertising and marketing to today's Boomer Consumer as well.

Introduction: The Most Powerful Communications Tool Ever

Sometimes the suggestion of incorporating storytelling to effectively connect with today's Boomer Consumer is met with exasperated looks and comments. "We're not in the days of Mark Twain, where someone can wax on about lazy days floating down the Mississippi; we're selling financial services to time-stressed Boomers," some marketers say. "We can't be telling sappy stories; we need to be rational and factual," add others.

Wren/Omnicom Group :: Jeff Yabuki/Fiserv :: David Yost/AmerisourceBergen :: Jim Young/Union Pacific :: Ed

But those time-stressed Boomers are still humans, with emotions and feelings and memories and ideas, ready and willing to hear and learn new things that could make their lives better and more interesting and rewarding. Why wouldn't you want to connect with them to provide them information about your products? Stories, anecdotes, and examples can be the easiest and best way to make those connections.

Interestingly, an increasing number of "experts" now espouse storytelling as the latest fad in communications. However, we think storytelling has been the most effective and powerful communications tool since humans learned how to talk. It was how knowledge was passed down from generation to generation before — and after — the development of written language. From Biblical tales of the Old and New Testaments to modern-day bestselling novels and blockbuster movies, stories and anecdotes serve to help us learn and reinforce life lessons. Using facts and figures to present a scientific and evidentiary based case is a fairly new development and really didn't start until the last several hundred years.

Stories, examples, and anecdotes work because people remember them. Aesop's Fables and the sayings of the Chinese philosopher Confucius are both now 2,500 years old. And for thousands of years, we've been telling and re-telling the stories found in the Bible. They are called "Bible stories," not "Bible facts." Stories endure. Facts are updated and replaced.

In the early days of TV advertising, the conventional wisdom on how to use the newfound ability to show and demonstrate the product or service was to rely on facts. A spokesperson or authority figure, often in a lab coat, held up the product and recited relevant specifics and figures. It wasn't until the early 1960s that TV advertising started using storytelling techniques. Bill Bernbach, of the advertising agency Doyle Dane Bernbach, realized that TV commercials offered the opportunity to tell stories in 60 seconds that engaged, delighted, and informed the viewer (now the standard is 30 or even 15 seconds). He saw commercials as mini-movies and created some of the most memorable TV campaigns of all time: VW's original Beetle ("Think Small"), Avis's "We Try Harder" and Life Cereal's "Mikey."

Zander/Motorola :: Jim Ziemer/Harley-Davidson :: John Zillmer/Allied Waste Inds :: Bill Zollars/YRC Worldwide

Since then, advertising has done a better job of using stories to present compelling information about products and services. As discussed in the last chapter, many times TV ads seem to be all about entertaining the viewer and not communicating anything. Therefore stories, examples, or anecdotes have to make a point, and not just entertain.

Advertising, Stories, and Boomers

In 2005 we developed two ads for a make-believe financial services firm, BMF Financial. We showed the ads to Boomers as part of a national quantitative study and asked them a series of questions about each. We wanted to learn what they thought about each ad, if they understood the message in each, and what they liked or disliked.

The ads were for a bank account designed especially for older consumers over 50. The first ad (left) has a picture of a piggy bank and the headline "Our Legacy Account rewards everyone over 50 for all those pennies they've saved." The copy is straightforward and factual, telling the reader that the Legacy Account "pays higher interest and gives you free checks, no ATM fees and a Safe Deposit Box."

The second ad (left) has a color picture of a man with salt-and-pepper hair, hugging a little girl at what appears to be a festival or event. The headline, "You might know a reason why our Legacy Account makes sense for you," is intentionally ambiguous about the relationship between the man and girl – he could be her father or her grandfather. The copy starts with, "Her name is Amy. You never thought she would impact your life as much as she has. Especially after all you've seen and done. But she means everything to you." Again, we were careful not to specify the relationship, in hopes that the reader would interpret the situation to fit their own life.

The copy goes on to say, "The Legacy Account at BMF is for people like you. People who want to make the most out of life without wasting time or money. People who want value and service from their financial institution after all these years." The copy then contains the information about the account features and benefits. No where in the ad do we specify an age requirement for the account.

In our national study, Boomers preferred the "Amy" ad by a three-to-one margin. They said it did a better job of getting their attention and was more interesting and informative.

In the study we allowed people to write in comments about what they especially liked or disliked about the ad. The "Piggy Bank" ad got very few positive comments, other than people acknowledging that it was straightforward and informative. The "Amy" ad garnered significantly more response, almost all positive. Interestingly, younger Boomer respondents identified the man as Amy's grandfather and older Boomers, those in their mid-to-late-50's, said the man was Amy's father.

Adding "Color" Between the Lines

Ever thought about how color influences your ads? Neither did we, until consumers started commenting about the use of bright colors in the "Amy" and other ads. It was unintentionally more vivid than the "Piggy Bank" ad and Boomer Consumers noticed it. We're planning on investigating the use of color in ads for older Boomers in future studies. Meanwhile, check out existing research and examples as to how older consumers process color at www.boomerconsumer.com. You might come up with some bright ideas for your ads!

Jason Alexander :: Adam Arkin :: Tom Arnold :: Rosanna Arquette :: Rowan Atkinson :: Dan Aykroyd :: Hank

Today advertisers can still use stories, examples, and anecdotes to draw the attention of and pull in readers. Nike recently ran a campaign for a line of women's exercise clothing. One ad featured a close-up of a woman's shoulder, with words following her contours and saying: "My shoulders aren't dainty, or proportional to my hips. Some say they are like a man's. I say, leave men out of it. They are mine. I made them in a swimming pool, then I went to yoga and made my arms. Just do it."

It isn't a story in the literal sense, but it is personal and engaging and much more than the standard beauty shot of a model wearing the product with the Nike logo.

Clearly there is some magic that stories, examples, and anecdotes have over consumers. It can be codified and put to use in marketing to today's Boomer Consumer.

Story Power

There are five reasons to use stories, examples, and anecdotes.

1. *Stories get your full attention.*

To process a story, you have to stop daydreaming and focus in on it. You *have* to pay attention. For example, in this book we've shared a story about a Boomer at the beginning of nearly every chapter. We've also used examples and shared anecdotes to help illustrate a point or provide context. You, as a reader, are more likely to retain and remember those sections than in lists such as this that simply provide information.

The human brain is an amazing multi-tasking parallel processor, like a Pentium Four taken to the trillionth power. We can operate a complex vehicle like a car, talk on the cell phone, eat a burrito, all the while looking for a place to park. We certainly multi-task when exposed to advertising, often ignoring it altogether. But we're more likely to pay attention when the ad tells us a story or shares an interesting example or anecdote that engages us directly.

Consider the Apple commercial that launched the "Mac" during the 1984 Super Bowl. It told a "1984-esque" story in a dramatic fashion. In fact, with that simple description, if you've seen the commercial, we may have jogged your memory and you can see it again now in your mind's eye. It's been over 20 years. Stories endure, don't they?

When someone's listening to a story, especially at the beginning, the brain engages full-time, and locks on exclusively to processing the tale. All multi-tasking stops.

2. Stories reach everyone.

Studies have been done that show people process information using their senses – what we see, hear, and feel. In his book *How to Make People Like You in 90 Seconds or Less*, Nicholas Boothman reports that half of us process information primarily based on what we see, 38% of us do it based primarily on what we feel, and 7% based on what we hear.

People process information differently. Some are "visual" and want to see the pictures in their minds, while others primarily focus through listening, feel, and intuition. Still others will watch you closely, noting you, the storyteller's, visual cues and body language.

This means you'll want to use descriptive, vivid language, to "hook" the visual folks. You'll also need sound-related references for the auditory information processors – "the engine in this new Lexus is so quiet you have to put your hand on the hood to make sure it is running." And for those who process based on how they feel, you'll need both physical description ("The community is nestled halfway up Hooker's Mountain, enabling homeowners to catch glimpses of Charlottesville and the valley every time they venture outside)" and engage the sensory ("The sensation [of the breath strip] is eye-opening and refreshing, lasting long after the instant it dissolves on your tongue").

By carefully constructing your story or anecdote, you can communicate effectively with just about everyone. As mentioned earlier in this book, the three rules of advertising are to:

Ellen Barkin :: Kim Basinger :: Angela Bassett :: Kathy Bates :: Jennifer Beals :: Ed Begley :: Shari Belafonte

- Get their attention
- Communicate something
- Persuade the audience to think, feel, or act differently

Stories enable you to effectively accomplish the first two steps.

Laugh Tracks

Even though he's getting older like the rest of the Boomers, Jerry Seinfeld is still funny.

Boomers still like a good laugh, but respond to humor differently than when they were younger. The evolution in appreciation of humor is natural and happens simply as a result of growing older. Humor that connects with today's Boomers is that of a Jerry Seinfeld or a George Carlin — observational, everyday things that make us laugh. It isn't raw, and doesn't rely on foul language, sexual references or put-downs.

Your message will be more effective with warm, gentle humor that uses irony, or is self-effacing.

---

3. Stories say a lot without saying a lot.

The story at the beginning of this chapter about Brad Lynch offered an impression of Brad and a sense of his success. But it never described him or told you his annual income. You infer things from stories, consciously or not.

For decades, advertisers have had to demonstrate things like trust, commitment, and integrity, without coming right out and saying that's what they're doing. By using a story, you can lay claim to the same thing. Subtle and skillfully crafted stories and anecdotes can reveal much about your product or service without hitting the customer over the head with it.

Both Home Depot and Lowe's are effective at "hammering" home messages of customer service. In the past they put real employees on camera and had them pledge their commitment to you, the customer. Depending on how sincere and honest they appear, they may or may not have been seen as believable. However, both now use commercials that show – rather than tell about - customer service.

One spot from Home Depot features a 40-something single mom with two teenage girls. Mom has decided she can do most of the fixing up of her home, with the help and guidance from the fine folks at Home Depot. Scene after scene depicts her hammering, measuring, sawing, and visiting Home Depot, where helpful employees point her in the right direction, demonstrate building techniques, or otherwise provide good customer service. She provides a running commentary on the process and ends with her hope that she's set a good example for her two girls and given them the sense that they can achieve anything. There is no overt claim by Home Depot about excellent customer service, they simply demonstrate it as part of the Mom's story.

In the Lowe's commercial mentioned in Chapter 3, a college-aged son returns home with a duffle bag of dirty laundry, only to find the washing machine and dryer on the curb as trash. He's relieved when he pulls in the driveway and sees the Lowe's truck unloading replacements. Mom and Dad tousle his hair and give him a hard time about only coming home to do his laundry. The announcer tells us Lowe's will deliver and install major appliances.

Once more, there is a demonstration of customer service instead of just an empty claim about it. That's what stories and anecdotes can do.

4. Stories trump facts every time.

The most successful and effective lawyers will tell you that they win their cases not by doing a better job of presenting the facts, but by telling a

Timothy Bottoms :: Lorraine Bracco :: Kenneth Branagh :: Benjamin Bratt :: Jeff Bridges :: Matthew Broderick

better story that fits the facts. Judges and juries want to do the right thing and sometimes the facts don't fit the story. If the story is more believable than the hard evidence, the story usually wins. Or as the celebrity attorney Johnnie Cochran said at the O.J. Simpson trial in the 1990s, "If the glove don't fit, you must acquit." Those words marked the beginning of a web of stories and anecdotes used to convince the jury that the facts didn't reveal what happened.

The same is true in marketing and advertising, especially with today's Boomer Consumers. For 40, 50, and now 60 years, Boomers have consumed millions of marketing messages. There is simply no way they can recall all the facts, but they can likely remember the stories. Earlier in this chapter we mentioned the Life Cereal commercial about "Mikey." Most who've seen that commercial clearly recall the three young boys eating breakfast, with the two older ones refusing to try the new cereal. Finally one boy pushes it towards youngest brother "Mikey" and says, "Let's get Mikey to try it, he hates everything." Mikey digs in, and the older boys are astonished that, "He likes it, he actually likes it!"

Parents and kids across America bought Life Cereal by the truckload, convinced that it has a taste even a kid like Mikey would like. That story was much more powerful than having an announcer tell the viewer that Life has a cinnamon and sugary taste kids will love. Those may be the facts, but until they are communicated effectively with a story or anecdote, few may remember or act upon them.

5. Stories involve the audience.

To get a message across without using a story or anecdote, a marketer has to make the facts, figures, and evidence fit into each audience member's existing set of beliefs. The marketer must do all the work, supplanting what's already in the audience member's head.

With a story, the marketer can ignite a spark – a memory or feeling - and the viewer, reader, or listener will do the work to apply the story to their specific situation. "Mikey" and the 1984 Apple spot are examples of this; people remember them even today, and they remember the

:: Albert Brooks :: Pierce Brosnan :: Sandra Bullock :: Delta Burke :: Nicolas Cage :: Kate Capshaw :: Drew

product as well. The best communications and communicators do that — involve the audience. They pull you in so you complete the thought or idea presented. It is ultimately how they persuade you to think, feel, or act differently.

Marketers and advertisers don't have to do all the work to make a point. Consider the best teacher or professor you ever had in high school or college. Not your favorite, but the best. The one who, when you went to their class, you enjoyed it and you learned. Even if you felt like doing something else.

Now ask yourself, why were they the best? What made them superior to other teachers or professors?

It was likely because they used stories, examples and anecdotes. They make the subject matter more interesting because they found ways to make it relevant and involving.

And, in making you think about that long-past teacher, we just ignited the spark. We asked a question and you completed a story. We don't even know the person's name, and don't have to because you are the one doing the remembering. You are doing the bulk of the work.

That's the power of story. And you can put it to use in marketing to today's Boomer Consumer.

Make It True If Not Real

Equally important is the fact that the story should ring true with consumers, even if you've made up portions. Of course, Mark Twain had the best advice — "If you tell the truth, you don't have to remember anything."

In advertising, a story doesn't need to be 100% accurate or even a verbatim recounting of an event (it is a "story" after all). It can be an extrapolation of a situation or a combination of several different happenings to make your point. But first and foremost it must be believable.

Carey :: Robert Carlyle :: Keith Carradine :: Jim Carrey :: Lynda Carter :: Dana Carvey :: Dan Castellaneta ::

Summary

The oldest and most effective technique in communications is to tell stories, use examples, and share anecdotes. Stories make advertising more powerful and memorable.

The key reasons stories work is that they:
1. Get your full attention.
2. Reach everyone.
3. Say a lot without saying a lot.
4. Trump facts every time.
5. Involve the audience.

Chapter 10
Rule 6: Understand My Changing Values

Bud Cort :: Kevin Costner :: Courteney Cox :: Cathy Lee Crosby :: Russell Crowe :: Tom Cruise :: Billy Crystal ::

Martha Madison is 49 and has worked full-time since she graduated college and got married. She's raised two boys, one in college and the other a senior in high school.

For most of her professional career, Martha worked in retail management with a regional department store. She rose from a junior buyer to store manager at one of the larger stores in a regional mall. The hours were long and she worked weekends and every holiday for years.

Then a national chain bought out the regional player and soon afterwards Martha was let go as part of a company-wide reduction. Although Martha still planned on working, she wanted a job where she felt she was making a difference. If she was going to log in all those hours, she felt, it should be at a place of employment that would make her feel good about herself.

Soon she found her dream job. Martha now runs the three Goodwill retail stores for in her area, and jumps out of bed every day to go to work.

Martha is like many Boomers at mid-life.

Introduction: Mid-Life Transitions

In Chapter 2, Boomer Psychology, we talked about the four different stages of a typical long life – Youth, Young Adult, Middle Age, and Old Age. We used an analogy of the four seasons, Spring, Summer, Fall, and Winter, each lasting about 20 years across a lifespan of some 80 or more years.

We also talked about how the underlying behavior of consumers during their first half of life, through Spring and Summer, seems rooted in satisfying the needs of the social self. During the second half of life, our behavior seems more focused on the needs of the inner self. We used the example of the underlying motivations of a 25-year old buying a BMW to impress others, while a 55-year-old purchases one because it makes them happy and cares less, if at all, about what others may think.

Tim Curry :: Jane Curtin :: Jaime Lee Curtis :: Joan Cusack :: William Dafoe :: Jeff Daniels :: Ted Danson ::

Aging and Changing Motivations

The Boomer Project tested out this theory of aging and changing behavior motivations. In a 2003 study, we asked all respondents ages 18-60 about their participation in a list of activities. We wanted to know if they felt they were doing these activities more or less often as compared to ten years ago. Our hypothesis was that older Boomers would say they are doing more inner-directed activities than socially-directed activities.

The following chart describes the results:

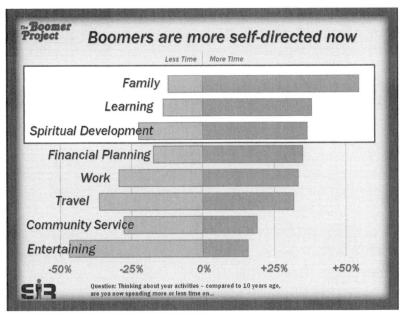

Source: The Boomer Project

Compared to ten years ago, older Boomers, those over 50 in this particular study, did say they are spending more time on things like Family, Learning and Spiritual Development. They are spending less time in the Community and Entertaining.

Those results prompted us to dig deeper. In a 2005 study of Boomers and younger adults, we explored the importance of different values. We asked people how important the values are in their life right now, on a scale from 1 to 10, with 1 being "Not Important at All" and 10 being "Very Important."

Here are the values we asked about (and they were presented in a random order to each respondent):

- Self-Respect
- Security
- Getting Fun & Enjoyment out of Life
- Being Well-Respected
- Self-Fulfillment
- Belonging
- Sense of Accomplishment
- Having Warm Relationships with Others

Unbeknownst to the respondents in the survey, these values can be grouped as follows:

Basic Values:

- Security
- Belonging
- Being Well-Respected

Social Values:

- Having Warm Relationships with Others
- Getting Fun & Enjoyment out of Life

Internal Values:

- Self-Fulfillment
- Self-Respect
- Sense of Accomplishment

After everyone rated each value on its relative importance to them right now, we then asked them to look over the list again and chose the one single value most important to them at this stage in their life.

The results were quite revealing.

About the same percentage of Young Adults, younger Boomers (those still in their 40s), and older Boomers (those over 50) identified one of the Basic Values as the most important to them right now. But that wasn't the case with the other two categories of values. More Young Adults and younger Boomers than older identified Social Values as the most important in their lives right now. Similarly, more older Boomers than younger in either category said the Internal Values were most important to them.

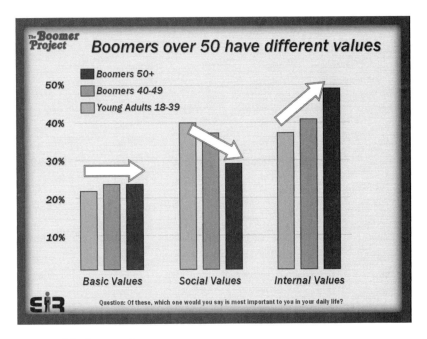

Source: The Boomer Project

Somewhere between their 40's and 50's, Boomers shift away from Social Values and towards Internal Values. It can best be explained as a Boomer growing out of focusing on "becoming someone" towards "being someone."

Marketers and advertisers must understand this shift to better connect with today's Boomer Consumer. A company or organization that thinks a 50-something Boomer is still the same self-absorbed, self-centered

Dreyfuss :: David Duchovny :: Julia Duffy :: Patrick Duffy :: Shelley Duvall :: Anthony Edwards :: David James narcissistic person from the 1960s, 70s or 80s could easily develop marketing messages that will terribly misfire. Remember the Lincoln Financial TV commercial described in Chapter 2, about the retired (and well-off) man teaching disabled kids how to ski? He was motivated to do it not because of what it said about him to others (outwardly-driven), but what it said about himself to himself (inwardly-driven).

This transition in life priorities is not unique to Boomers; it's a natural part of what happens when we grow older. Every generation goes through the same phases.

What it Means to Grow Old

Still the "Golden Years" for Boomers will be different from the past, thanks in part to better understanding among scientists and psychologists as to how the brain works. Interestingly, the foundations for most of today's theories of cognitive development comes from the work of Sigmund Freud and Erik Erikson, both of whom basically viewed life after 50 as one phase, without any "new" developments in the way the brain works.

The Mature Mind, by Dr. Gene Cohen, debunks this theory and describes the positive power of the aging brain. Rather than automatically going into a slow, steady decline, in many ways the older brain is a smarter brain. And it certainly is a wiser brain.

With age comes wisdom may sound like an old bromide but in truth is a scientific fact. That is essentially the message of Dr. Cohen's book. The director of the Center on Aging at George Washington University, he has spent his professional life investigating "successful aging" in older men and women. Through his work as a psychiatrist and gerontologist, he concluded that cognitive development continues throughout life, not just during childhood and adolescence. Older people, even after age 85, still learn, develop, and process information in ways we simply didn't understand before. Which is good news; there is new wisdom that only comes with age.

Elliott :: Cary Elwes :: Emilio Estevez :: Erik Estrada :: Morgan Fairchild :: Farrah Fawcett :: Sally Field ::

Dr. Cohen outlines four distinct development phases of late life: midlife reevaluation, liberation, summing up, and encore. People enter and pass through these phases based on inner drives, desires, and urges that come and go throughout life. Cohen calls these drives the "Inner Push" and says it is the fuel motivating development. His four phases are more fluid than phases one might experience during youth, as he has concluded people later in life vary widely in every conceivable way.

Phase	Age Range	Characteristics
Midlife Reevaluation	40's to mid-60s	Not a crisis, but a quest; searching for true meaning in life
Liberation	Late 50's to mid-70's	"If not now, when?"
Summing Up	Late 60's to mid-80's	Recapitulation, resolution and review, includes desire to give back
Encore	Mid-80's on	Desire to go on, keep going, not to stop

Source: The Mature Mind

A new concept introduced by Dr. Cohen is "developmental intelligence." This is the combination of wisdom, judgment, perspective, and vision one develops later in life. It is characterized by three types of thinking and reasoning typically developed after age 50 or so: **relativistic thinking** (recognizing that knowledge is relative and not absolute); **dualistic thinking** (the ability to uncover and resolve contradictions in opposing and seemingly incompatible views); and **systemic thinking** (being able to see the larger picture, to distinguish between the forest and the trees).

He tells a great story of an older couple coming to Washington, D.C. to visit their daughter. They get off the Metro at a station a mile or so from their daughter's Georgetown home and plan to take a taxi. But it is pouring down rain and there are no cabs to be found. Dad, age 78, sees a pizza parlor on the corner and has an idea. Without saying a word to his wife, he ushers her in and asks if the pizza parlor delivers. When he learns they do, he orders a pizza to be sent to his daughter's address with the caveat that he and his wife get delivered as well.

Dr. Cohen points out that Dad's solution to the problem of getting to his daughter's house in a driving rainstorm required completely new and novel thinking. With age comes wisdom indeed.

He goes on to point out that in youth we tend to want our answers in black and white, right or wrong. We usually prefer any answer to none at all. With age we develop our capacity to accept uncertainty, to admit that answers are often relative, and to suspend judgment for a more careful evaluation of opposing views. All of which are a true measure of our developmental intelligence.

BoomBox

Men and Growing Old

On April 12, 2004, Billy Crystal was a guest on Dave Letterman's Late Show. It was Dave's 57th birthday. Billy was also 57 at the time. Both are Boomers, and because it was Dave's birthday they started talking about growing old and what that means for them. Billy told stories about getting up in the middle of the night to go to the bathroom, and "peeing in Morse Code." Dave spoke about how difficult it is for him to get everything working when he gets up in the morning. They laughed. The audience laughed. Everyone had a good time.

That date, April 12, 2004, should go down in history as the "tipping point" when it became okay for Boomers to grow older. That's because two Boomer-age entertainers, Dave Letterman and Billy Crystal, both of whom have ridiculed and stereotyped "senior" citizens as part of their routines, found that they could comfortably talk about the realities of aging in a funny, self-deprecating manner. They weren't disparaging. They were charming and self-effacing.

French :: Matt Frewer :: Peter Gallagher :: James Gandolfini :: Andy Garcia :: Teri Garr :: Brad Garrett :: An-

This shift from making fun of this object called "old people" to laughing at themselves and their age-related physical changes is significant. What once was funny at other people's expense was now funny at our own expense.

In October that same year, comedian Richard Lewis was a guest and started talking with Dave about how his body had become a mushy mess since he had turned 50. Dave joked that he had recently gotten up in the middle of the night and had passed a mirror and thought an old, naked guy had broken into his house. Now "old" is funny... and respectable.

The Mature Mind also presents a new approach to aging, differing even from *Successful Aging*, a popular book that focuses on minimizing decline. Instead, Dr. Cohen demonstrates how older brains can experience positive changes, even after age 85.

He also recognizes the importance of brain fitness and recommends five activities to help keep the juices flowing: mental exercises, physical exercise, challenging leisure activities, achieving mastery of interests, and establishing strong social networks. The mental exercises can be as simple as doing crossword puzzles or sudoku regularly, or they could be formal, multi-dimensional exercises using software tools.

Dr. Cohen presents a compelling case for staying creative later in life, by doing things that challenge the mind and imagination. He and other researchers found that older people who signed up for and participated in a community-based art program were healthier one year later, had had fewer doctor visits, used fewer medications, felt less depressed, were less lonely, and had higher morale.

Thinking of older consumers as mentally declining is doing them a great disservice. Boomers will not go quietly into the night, sitting on their rocking chairs sipping lemonade. They will stay bright, engaged, focused and, as needed, vocal, as they maintain mental vitality for decades to come.

thony Geary :: Richard Gere :: Melissa Gilbert :: Robin Givens :: Danny Glover :: Whoopie Goldberg :: Jeff

Changing Values in Marketing and Advertising

So what does "being someone" – rather than "becoming someone" – mean in terms of marketing and advertising messages? Many marketers in the travel industry have already figured out that older consumers have different values. Those targeting a clientele ages 50 and beyond tend to communicate different attributes and benefits of their property or attraction.

For example, Le Meridien Hotels and Resorts runs a print ad featuring a close-up photo of an older woman's face, as if she's luxuriating at a pool or spa. The headline says simply "Land in a place where you can just be." The message is that older consumers, today's Boomer Consumer, for instance, can come to Le Meridien and not worry about any activities, events, pressure, children (implied), or anything else that could get in the way of relaxation.

Relaxation is an attractive benefit for today's Boomer. In fact, it's the main idea behind a travel ad for the state of North Carolina promoting their pristine beaches. The visual is a single glass door standing by itself on the beach. Ostensibly it's from an office building and written on the door are the words, "Relaxation Clinic." The only other copy on the ad is "North Carolina. A better place to be."

Once more, a travel marketer is not selling things to do, places to see, or people to visit. Instead they are offering up self-fulfillment and self-actualization in a tranquil setting. Picture yourself here. Literally. Doing whatever you need to do to just be. Including doing nothing.

Another marketer who understands today's Boomer Consumer is Unilever's Dove brand of skin and beauty aids. Boomers may recall the days of the Dove bar with "one-quarter cleansing cream" that won't dry your skin. Now the Dove brand has a wide range of products to clean, replenish, renew, and invigorate skin and hair. (Recall we talked about one of their lines, the "Pro-Age" products, back in Chapter 7.)

In late 2004 Dove launched a new advertising campaign called "Campaign for Real Beauty" (www.campaignforrealbeauty.com).

Goldblum :: John Goodman :: Gilbert Gottfried :: Nancy Lee Grahn :: Kelsey Grammer :: Hugh Grant :: Pam

Dove challenged the existing notions that beauty is best defined as a 20-something model with perfect skin and no body fat. In contrast, their advertising featured everyday people of varying ages, sizes, and ethnic origins. The initial campaign consisted of billboards, print ads, and TV commercials presenting a woman with the question, "What do you think?" and two choices. For example, one photo was of an older woman with long gray hair. "What do you think?" was followed with "Gray?" or "Gorgeous?"

Another showed a red-headed freckled face woman with "Flawed?" or "Flawless?" Yet another featured a skinny African-American woman with "Half empty?" or "Half full?"

The impact was immediate and tremendous. Dove has been very effective in changing perceptions about "beauty" since they began the campaign, and sales of their health and beauty products jumped 12.5%, to $535 million in 2005 from $476 million the previous year, according to Information Resources Inc., which tracks consumer packaged goods. Considering that Revlon launched and then dropped their Vital Radiance line over the same period due lack of sales, Dove obviously struck a responsive chord and understands the changing values of Boomer Consumers.

Women and Growing Old

On Tuesday, December 6, 2005, Katie Couric, then age 48, did a story on "Today" called "50 is the New 30." As with the acceptance of growing older by David Letterman and Billy Crystal, this date is one that women might say the rules changed for them. The story featured supermodels Cheryl Tiegs, 58, and Christie Brinkley, 51, talking about how "50 is the new 30" and that cosmetic companies are using older models and actresses in their ads to appeal to aging Baby Boomers. Christie discussed

Grier :: Melanie Griffith :: Arye Gross :: Christopher Guest :: Steve Guttenberg :: Jasmine Guy :: Mark Hamill

how Revlon's products are now scientifically designed to deflect light from wrinkles, resulting in a younger appearance.

That's when Katie said, "I have such mixed feelings about this; I'm so happy that people are embracing women as they age, but are they really embracing the aging process? In other words, is this about women in their 50s trying to look 30? I mean, everyone wants to look attractive, but I just wish that that didn't necessarily mean no wrinkles, you know, because I think that's a sign of experience and wisdom and the fact that you've lived. So do you guys ever think that not everybody has to look like they're 30 to be really beautiful?"

According to Katie, real beauty isn't tied to one's age. She likely wouldn't have had such epiphanies at age 38. She wasn't "mature enough" to come to these conclusions back then. But she is now.

Cheryl Tiegs answered Katie by asserting that, "I don't know if we're trying to look like we're 30, I just think we're doing the best we can with our age and with what we have. I think the days of plastic surgery, pulling everything back, getting rid of every single line and wrinkle, are over."

Cheryl went on to say, "Women today are doing something that's never been done in the history of civilization, and that's looking fabulous until the day you die."

Then Christie said, "I think that 50-year-old women today have very full, interesting lives...we're comfortable being our age, we don't want to be just forgotten, we don't want to keep seeing 20-year-olds as the standard for vibrant, important people — we're vibrant, important ourselves."

Now, if only marketers would listen....

:: Linda Hamilton :: Harry Hamlin :: Tom Hanks :: Daryl Hannah :: Woody Harrelson :: Ed Harris :: David Has-

Social vs. Personal Benefits

The Dove campaign takes on a social cause by trying to change perceptions of beauty in American culture. Other marketers, like Starbucks, have embraced the environment and gone "Green," with recycled cups and organically-grown coffee.

We anticipate this trend to increase in coming years as more Boomers reach the stage of life where they start to wonder about their legacy. They will want to leave the world a better place, whether they are coming full circle from the idealistic late 1960s and early 70s or simply experiencing later-in-life altruism. Boomers will respond better to companies with a social conscience than those that simply "consume."

However, the "Boomer dance" can be complicated. On the one hand they want to feel good about doing business with you and feel like you share their values about the planet and society. On the other, they want to know how your product or service will make them feel better about themselves, personally. At heart, they are still consumers, with that all-important question: "What's in it for me?"

The latter "me" is different from that of the "Me Decade." It represents a search for self-fulfillment, self-respect, and self-actualization. Make sure your socially responsible product, service, or marketing effort has something for the Boomer Consumer's "me." We'll cover how to do that in the next chapter.

Summary

Boomers at mid-life are evolving from "becoming someone" to "being someone." Understanding this shift in values is important as it will require different approaches to marketing and advertising.

- The payoff needs to be inwardly focused (you'll feel good about yourself), not focused on social aspects (your friends will think you're cool).

selhoff :: Teri Hatcher :: Patricia Heaton :: Mariel Hemingway :: Marilu Henner :: Barbara Hershey :: Jan

- The way older minds work and process information provides opportunities for marketers to engage older consumers in new and different ways.

- Boomers, who are reaching the phase of life where they are starting to think about their legacy, will look for products and services from marketers that help them in their quest towards self-fulfillment and self-actualization.

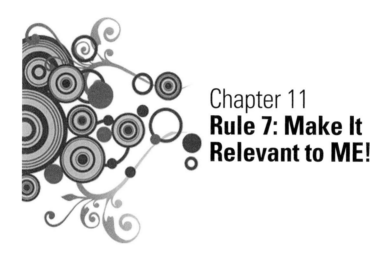

Chapter 11
Rule 7: Make It Relevant to ME!

Hunter :: William Hurt :: Olivia Hussey :: Anjelica Huston :: Timothy Hutton :: Jeremy Irons :: Samuel L. Jack-

W hen *Art Trice was growing in Missouri he was just like all of his friends. He drank Coca-Cola, wore Levi's jeans, had Converse sneakers and used Crest toothpaste. His favorite cookies were Oreos and he liked to eat at McDonald's. He viewed all of those decisions as choices he had made – Coke over Pepsi, Levi's over Lee Jeans, Converse over PF Fliers, Crest over Colgate, Oreos over Chips Ahoy, and McDonald's over Burger King.*

Now that Art is 47 he finds himself drinking diet Coke with Lime, wearing Levi's 560 Loose Fit jeans, wearing Nike Shock sneakers, using Crest Baking Soda and Whitening toothpaste, enjoying Uh-Oh Oreos and only eating the premium salads at McDonald's when his kids want to eat there. At one level, Art still believes he is making choices of one brand over another – Coke over Pepsi and so forth. But in truth, he isn't.

Art's choices are not between competitors, but within the brands he has always bought. That's because those marketers, and others, have tapped into a generational trait among Boomers of wanting to make all purchase decisions relevant to themselves personally. These days Art doesn't think of himself as a Coke drinker, he's a diet Coke with Lime drinker. He doesn't wear Nike sneakers, he wears Nike Shock sneakers. He's not like everyone else who buys Crest toothpaste; he only buys the Baking Soda and Whitener version. In fact, put together all the unique combinations of product decisions Art makes, and he's not like anyone else. He's unique.

Just like all Boomers.

Introduction: What's In It for Me?

In Chapter 4 we discussed the generational traits or characteristics that can be found in many of the 78 million Boomers. These traits were formed as a result of Boomers coming of age during the same time in history and therefore also experiencing the same general American culture and society. Three things especially united them: the nationalistic pride and focus that persisted after World War II as America became an undisputed world leader, the broad and consistent reach of television, and Dr. Benjamin Spock's approach to child-rearing. These experiences

son :: Susan Saint James :: Bruce Jenner :: Ann Jillian :: Don Johnson :: Grace Jones :: Tommy Lee Jones ::

formed the glue for the Boomer generation, an effect similar to the Great Depression and World War II on previous generations.

One of the key traits Boomers formed as a result of coming of age in the late 1950s, 60s, and early 70s was what we call "self" centered. From being self-indulged as children to being self-absorbed as young adults to now becoming self-fulfilled and self-actualized, Boomers have always found a way to put themselves first. As discussed in Chapter 4, Boomers were raised in child-centric households, where children were not only seen and heard, but cherished. As children and teenagers, Boomers saw parents, businesses, colleges, and social institutions bend to their will while attempting to placate, market, or educate them. No surprise they came to believe they were the center of it all.

It's All About 78 Million

The PBS documentary, *Boomer Century*, produced by and featuring *Age Wave* author Dr. Ken Dychtwald, identifies four traits found in Boomers: idealism, anti-authoritarianism, eagerness to embrace change, and self-empowerment. We think that's as good a list we've seen, although the underlying question fueling those traits in Boomers is, "What's in it for me?"

Boomers may have formed this underlying "self" focus as a defensive mechanism to deal with their sheer numbers. Rare is the Boomer who was an only child, given that some 90% of the women who could have children had, according to the U.S. Census, an average of 4.0 across the 18-year span of the cohort. So from the early days of vying for attention among elder or younger siblings, Boomer children had to identify, develop, and articulate their individuality. Finding themselves in classrooms with 35 or more students, in schools with larger and larger populations, young Boomers had to obey the rules and conform, while sorting out what they could think or feel or do to be unique as individuals.

The reality was that even if your talents, abilities, and looks made you stand out in the crowd, there were 78 million other Boomers, an

Hugh Laurie :: Jet Li :: Jane Kaczmarek :: Carol Kane :: Julie Kavner :: Diane Keaton :: Michael Keaton ::

unprecedented number and a *lot* of competition. Even if you were "one in a million," the fact is there are 78 more Boomers exactly like you. As a result, the desire to be unique and noticed has driven Boomers to be "self" centered throughout their lives. Marketers should understand this, especially since, as discussed in the last chapter, today's older Boomer Consumer is more motivated by internal, inwardly-focused values than by the social, or outwardly-focused values of youth. Marketers positioning their goods and services for "everyone" will not be as successful as those who have structured their communications to address, "What's in this for me, personally?"

Following the Parade

In the early 1990s, the clothing brand GAP began an advertising campaign featuring famous celebrities. In the commercials, an actor, musician, or other celebrity talked about their approach to the craft and what makes them unique. At the end they would say something like, "And my khakis are GAP" or, "and my jeans are GAP." The message was that if you wanted to be unique and an individual, like this celebrity, then you should wear GAP clothes.

It was a brilliant approach to take with the Boomer generation, then ranging in age from their late 20's- mid 40's. In fact, during that time the white-collar work force daily "uniform" underwent a change as "Casual Fridays" and "Business Casual" became the norm. By the late 1990s one could walk into almost any office building in America and find the male Boomer workforce no longer wearing coats and ties, but clad in identical GAP khakis. It was still a "uniform," but the GAP advertising had convinced each individual that their khakis were a demonstration of uniqueness and individuality.

It is remarkable how GAP so successfully tapped into the psyche of Boomers, mining the individuality vein. Yet it is also disturbing (and somewhat ironic) that Boomer men were walking around, convinced they were projecting their individual style by wearing exactly the same thing. And if you couldn't afford GAP brand khakis, you bought knockoffs sold at discount stores.

Craig Kilborn :: Val Kilmer :: Natassia Kinski :: Kevin Kline :: Lisa Kudrow :: Cheryl Ladd :: Christine Lahti ::

If GAP had run ads showing groups of men wearing their khakis and made claims that "everyone has them," they would have had nowhere near the level of success. Boomers, striving to fulfill that need for "self" centeredness, would have responded to such advertising with "Well, I'm not *everybody*. I'm *ME*."

Boomers will not join the parade just because there is a parade. On their own, they have to conclude that they want to march and go in the same direction as the parade, and just because others are going the same way, that doesn't mean Boomers are following them. They just happen to be going in the same direction, that's all.

A more recent example of tapping into the "Me" Boomer mindset is iPod music devices. To date, Apple has sold over 100 million iPods, and not just to teenagers. Boomers have been buying them as well. Yet Apple hasn't marketed iPods to anyone other than teenagers and young adults. Nonetheless, Boomers love them.

Yet iPod users could be mistaken for "Pod" people. The telltale sign is the ubiquitous white bud dangling from the ears. In fact, every one of those 100 million iPods is essentially identical when it comes to those white ear buds. Walk into any health and fitness facility and you can see ten or twenty people lined up on the treadmills or stair climbers with those white ear buds. They all look identical. The same. Yet not a single one of them feels that way. That's because each one of them is listening to their own selection of music. The first person may be tuned into a classical piece while the other is plugged into a hip-hop song. No one is the same. Everyone is different.

iPods are the perfect product for today's Boomer Consumer: cool, hip, youthful and personalized. Every one's alike, but no two are exactly the same.

The Do-It-For-Me Generation?

Both Home Depot and Lowe's recently announced that their "do it for you" business is growing twice as fast as their traditional "do it yourself" business. Seems older Boomers aren't as interested in swinging a hammer as having someone else do it for them.

The $110 billion home maintenance and home improvement categories are poised to explode (or "boom," if you will) over the next 20 years as Boomers grow weary of the wear and tear on their bodies when they do all the work themselves. As of now, Home Depot provides 24 "Do It for You" (DIFY) services, including painting. Lowe's tops that with 40 DIFY services.

It is interesting that, beyond these two big box retailers, the home maintenance, repair and improvement category doesn't, as of yet, have a national company or franchise that provides reliable, reasonable services. Sears attempted to do that with appliance repair. But no one is offering to clean the gutters, organize the garage, cut the grass, paint the spare bedroom, mend the fence gate, or assemble the storage closet.

That is a trend to watch — and capitalize on.

Marketing to Me

Marketers and advertisers need to understand this mindset to connect with today's Boomer Consumer, who wants the product or service to be relevant to them, personally. A commercial from Lincoln Financial, whose other TV spot was discussed earlier in the book, tells the story of a 60-something man, who owns an exotic car repair shop. He is talking with a younger fellow who says, "So you're finally selling the place."

Shelley Long :: Julia Louis-Dreyfus :: John Lovitz :: Rob Lowe :: Susan Lucci :: Ralph Maccio :: Norm MacDon-

The man replies, "Yes, I just finally had to pursue my dream before I get too old to enjoy it." They talk further about the "new guy" buying the shop and that he'll do a good job.

The scene changes and the "new guy" pulls up and gets out of this car. He, too, is 60-something years old. The younger fellow says to him, "So, you bought this place?" The "new guy" says, "Yes, I figured I had to pursue my dream before I got too old to enjoy it."

Yet they are both approximately the same age! Once more, the folks at Lincoln Financial demonstrated that they understand the thinking of today's Boomer Consumer. It's perfectly fine that one man is giving up the repair shop to pursue his dream while the other is buying it so he can follow his. They both get to go after their respective dreams. The commercial makes an important emotional connection with Boomers.

The commercial also *tells a story*, as discussed in Chapter 9. One doesn't have to own a repair shop, or even want to buy one, to get the point about pursuing individual dreams. They make it easy for the viewer to figure out the rest.

Even marketers selling mass appeal products and services need to frame their message in the context of addressing that underlying Boomer question: What's in it for me? When we're conducting seminars or workshops with marketers, we advise them to be careful in using language to describe the popularity of their product or service. Even if almost every single person in American already consumes and loves your product or service, don't tell that to Boomers in hopes of getting them to try or buy. They have been marketed to since they were five years old and are the most experienced, jaded consumers of advertising and marketing messages on the planet. As we've said, their first response when they hear "everybody" in any marketing message is to think, "I'm not everybody. I'm ME."

Instead, we tell seminar attendees, a better approach is to talk about the types of people who try or buy your product or service. Describe the buyer, or tell a story about them that shares who they are, their attitudes and values, their interests and life styles, or their life stage. Paint a picture of the consumer for your product or service so the Boomer can decide on their own if you've described something they can relate to. If the Boomer feels that they are indeed like the consumer you've depicted, then they will become interested in your product or service. This is a much more effective approach than simply making the claim that "everybody" likes your product or service.

A growing number of marketers are realizing that a good way to attract Boomers is to *personalize the product or service*. You can get custom-built bicycles, shoes, clothes, cars, kitchens, and checking accounts. A recent *Wall Street Journal* article reported that resorts and spas are expanding exclusive perks found in the higher-priced rooms throughout the "public" areas of the property – special sections on the beach, at the spa, in the restaurant, at the golf course. That way the guests paying more for their stay get added amenities and benefits, allowing for a more personalized experience.

Boomers also want to answer "What's in it for me?" by determining for themselves what they perceive as the benefits of your product or service. If you tell them what the benefit is, it should be talked about in such a way that they can modify and personalize it, like Lincoln Financial helping people pursue their dreams. Dreams, obviously, are as individual as snowflakes.

The Lighthouse Effect: Beam Me Up

It becomes more complicated if you are selling something more tangible, like condominium living in a new downtown, urban development. Empty Nest Boomers are an ideal target audience for developers creating these "New Urbanism" mixed-use properties. The benefits could include things like no maintenance living, and proximity to work, restaurants, retail, and medical and other services. On the other hand, another key audience segment for these new developments is young, unmarried, and married professionals without kids. The benefits of living in such a development for this segment are different from that of the Boomers.

The younger adults are interested in living in a cool, hip place, near the vibrant night life. They want the address because of what it would say about them to their friends, peers, and coworkers. As we've discussed in the last chapter, Boomers Consumers are less interested in what anyone else might think about living in the development, but how it makes them feel about themselves.

If you were the developer or real estate firm with the task of promoting the property and couldn't afford two different marketing campaigns, what could you do?

One answer would be to focus on the physical attributes of the development and not the benefits. Describe the location and the amenities of the property itself. Let the readers of the ad or brochure, or the viewers of the TV commercial, picture themselves in the setting and ascribe to it the benefits most meaningful to them.

We call this the "Lighthouse" approach. A beacon or lighthouse out at sea calls attention to itself by showing off its most noticeable attribute – a bright light. Each passing vessel that sees the light derives its own benefit depending on the weather, time of day, and condition of the seas.

Your marketing and advertising to Boomer Consumers can take a similar approach. Simply present your bright light, your best attribute, and let the reader or viewer decide the benefit most relevant to them. Let *them* answer the question, "What's in it for me?" In most cases, they're going to do it anyway.

Summary

When connecting with Boomer Consumers, the most important question marketers and advertisers need to address is, "What's in it for me?"

- Raised as part of the largest generational cohort in history, Boomers have long strived for ways to protect and cherish their individuality. That underlying desire means they are less likely to respond to claims using words like "everybody" or "everyone."

- Apple's iPod is a current example of a product that taps into that mindset. In one sense, every iPod is exactly the same, down to the white ear buds plugged into the device. But a roomful of iPod users don't feel at all alike. That's because they are all listening to music that they've selected individually. No two iPods are the same.

- Boomers want to be able to find themselves in your messages, and will more readily relate to them if you communicate what type of people try and buy your product or service. You can describe them demographically or psychographically by their lifestyle trends, or more generally by life style or life stage. In any event, paint a picture and let the Boomer Consumer put themselves in it...or not.

- Use the "Lighthouse" approach to connect with Boomers. Put forth your best attribute and let *them* determine the benefit based on their current needs and wants.

Chapter 12
Rule 8: Play in the Gray

D r. Karen Deekens, 58, is a sociologist and the director of research at a regional marketing research firm. During her career she has worked in advertising agencies and at large corporations like Colgate and AT&T. Karen's entire career has been in the marketing research business, and she has been involved in enough research projects to have learned a few things about consumer behavior.

Karen has often found herself called upon to conduct marketing research among physicians and others in the medical profession. "It's almost impossible to do research with doctors," she says. "That's because the answer to any question posed to a doctor starts with, 'It depends.'"

In Karen's experience, doctors who deal with patient care have seen it all – therapies that work for one patient don't work for another. Symptoms found in one case don't appear in another seemingly identical case. Physicians learn that every patient is indeed unique and therefore answers to questions about patient care or therapies or pharmaceuticals or anything related to medicine must start with a qualifier: It depends.

Today's older Boomer Consumers are at a stage of cognitive development where that's basically how they respond to advertising and marketing. Nothing is black and white anymore. Everything is a shade of gray.

Introduction: Assuming the Position

In the advertising and marketing world, we often talk about how a company is "positioning" its product or service. This means how the company wants the consumer or customer to ultimately think or feel about their product or service. Companies and organizations hire firms like Boomer Project partner firm, SIR Research, to survey and study consumers to find out how they perceive a product or service and to learn how the consumer positions the product or service in their own minds. Ideally, the organization's chosen position is the same one held in the consumer's mind. But that's in a perfect world.

With today's Boomer Consumer, it is important to chose a position and communicate it in a "Conditional" manner instead of an "Absolute" manner. We'll talk about each of those approaches; then we'll share why today's Boomers will respond better to Conditional positioning.

North :: Chris Noth :: Rosie O'Donnell :: Gary Oldman :: Lena Olin :: Edward James Olmos :: Tatum O'Neal ::

Absolute vs. Conditional Positioning

Back in the early 1980s, Fred Smith started an overnight delivery business called Federal Express. Typical of advertising for a brand new concept, FedEx used humor to get your attention and then showed how they solve the problem. The early TV advertising from FedEx usually featured distraught businessmen and women waiting for a delivery that never comes. One commercial showed a man making hand shadows on the projection screen because his slides failed to arrive in time for his important meeting.

The message from FedEx ended with a strong, clear, superlative claim: "When it absolutely, positively has to be there overnight." They then supported that claim with a guarantee, to help make it believable. Not too long after FedEx began, the entrenched leader in delivery, UPS, developed a similar overnight delivery business and began advertising it to businesspeople. Their tagline was, "We run the tightest ship in the shipping business," and provided proof by showing how particular they are about clean trucks, uniforms, staying on schedule, and other operational efficiencies.

From an advertising standpoint, though, the UPS tagline was making what we call an "Absolute" claim: you either agree with it or not. There is no middle ground. It wasn't *"You'll think* we run the tightest ship in the shipping business." It was a declarative statement of absolute fact.

Quite often in advertising and marketing it makes sense to use the Absolute approach. Absolute positions tend to be about the company or organization, or are product-centric, and are rational and logical. If, for example, you make lawn mowers and tractors, then reliability and performance are the key benefits sought by purchasers of such equipment. In that case, a position that "Nothing runs like a Deere" for the John Deere brand certainly makes sense. You, as the target audience, can decide for yourself whether you agree with it or not.

The most believable Absolute positions are held by the established leaders in a category or industry. John Deere is the top player in lawn tractors and can make Absolute claims until someone unseats them. The older

Boomer readers will recall the seemingly outlandish claims made by a young Cassius Clay (later Muhammad Ali) in the 1960s that, "I am the greatest." Hard to believe at first, but he ultimately proved himself accurate and won over most of America and nearly all of his fights.

Absolute positioning comes with one major risk. You could be unseated by a competitor, which could prove embarrassing. Or you could fail to deliver against your promise. In the 1980s British Airways said they were "The world's favourite airline." Once they made such a claim, in order for it to stay believable they had to consistently deliver. They stopped using the tagline in the mid-1990s.

Mercedes-Benz used the positioning line, "Engineered like no other car in the world" through most of the 1980s and early 1990s. Then Lexus came along with their "Relentless pursuit of perfection" campaign which featured their unending commitment to details: they even use gold in the triggering mechanism for the airbag. In short order, Lexus made the Mercedes positioning less believable.

At the other end of the positioning spectrum are "Conditional" claims. Conditional claims are often consumer-centric and emotional instead of rational. If Absolute claims are statements about the organization from the organization's point of view, Conditional claims are statements about the consumer or customer from their point of view.

Let's go back to our example of UPS. While they still may operate "the tightest ship in the shipping business," that isn't what they are telling us in their advertising. Instead, they ask, "What can brown do for you?" The answer is, "it depends" (wonder if a physician heads up their advertising?). "What can brown do for you" is a classic example of a Conditional claim. It isn't so much about UPS as it is about the customer. It's emotional and not rational. The answer does indeed depend on the individual and specific needs of the customer. It's relative, not absolute.

These days Mercedes has replaced their "Engineered like no other car in the world," with the tag line "Unlike any other." But now it is a softer, less specific relative claim that the consumer has to evaluate against what they think and feel about all other cars. It's less about what Mercedes thinks about itself and more about what the consumer thinks about Mercedes.

Still another example of Absolute vs. Conditional is BMW. For years it has been "The ultimate driving machine." This is perhaps the definitive Absolute positioning: about the car not the consumer, very rational ("machine") and absolute: "ultimate." Now compare that to Volkswagen's tagline of "Drivers wanted." That is about the consumer, not the company, emotional and conditional. If you consider yourself a "driver," then this may be the car for you.

Boomer Women are headed to Mars, Boomer Men to Venus

Boomer women at age 50 and beyond are getting more in touch with their masculine side. Boomer men over 50 are becoming more feminine. Here's the surprise: both are normal human developments.

As David Wolfe points out on his Ageless Marketing blog, Carl Jung observed the fact that adult males in midlife or older get more in touch with their feminine side — their anima. In contrast, in midlife women begin to reflect more of their masculine side — their animus. Since the Boomer majority rule the marketplace (as they have for 40 years), it's no surprise that society is becoming more androgynous and sex identity less important.

Think of the stereotypes we know so well: "tough old grandma" and "gentle old granddad." Those stereotypes are based on biological changes in older people. In his book, *The Irritable Male Syndrome*, Jed Diamond points out that both men and women have naturally occurring estrogen and testosterone levels in their bodies. As women pass through menopause their estrogen levels decrease relative to their natural testosterone levels. As men

:: Bronson Pinchot :: Joe Piscopo :: Brad Pitt :: Mary Kay Place :: Markie Post :: Kelly Preston :: Victoria Princi-

reach their late 50's and beyond, their testosterone levels decrease relative to their estrogen levels. Diamond likes to say, "Men get more 'esty' and women get more 'testy.'"

All kidding aside, there are implications for marketers. Maybe it's time for "the softer side of Sears" to start showing up in the Craftsman tools department. And "built Ford tough" could apply to sedans in addition to trucks. In other words, traditional gender cues are less important for Boomers at this stage.

Boomers are Gray Now

Across the four phases of life, Youth, Young Adulthood, Middle Age and Old Age, as discussed in Chapter 2, cognitive development changes and evolves as we grow older. By the time someone reaches late life, starting in their 60's and beyond, the world is no longer a place filled with blacks and whites. Instead, everything is seen as a shade of gray. As David Wolfe writes in *Ageless Marketing*, "older consumers come to accept that the irony that there is some good in every bad and some bad in every good."

A few years ago, during the 2004 presidential campaign between John Kerry and George W. Bush, we worked with a small advertising agency run by some older Boomers. William was 58 years old and a lifelong conservative and Republican. Pete was a few years older and a lifelong liberal and Democrat. Despite their differing political views, William and Pete worked quite well together on a major project. Every once in a while they would poke and prod each other about the other's wayward leanings, but they never got into any heated and emotional exchanges.

We were in our mid-40's and wondered how they could get along so well despite their different political persuasions. Pete told us, "It's simple. I have my point of view and William has his. Mine works for me and it clearly doesn't work for William. The same can be said for his point of view and me. I could never accept it. That doesn't make him wrong or me wrong. We're just different."

pal :: Bill Pullman :: Dennis Quaid :: Randy Quaid :: Aiden Quinn :: Phylicia Rashad :: John Ratzenberger ::

Pete and William accepted their political differences and didn't let them get in the way of their professional lives. They were able to table those differences when it came to work. That ability is a learned behavior that only comes with time. If Pete and William were in their 20's, they would have argued night and day, with each trying to persuade the other to switch points of view. We doubt they could have separated their political selves from their work selves.

This ability to juggle different aspects of beliefs to get a job done is a sign of maturity. In fact, Dr. Gene Cohen, author of *The Mature Mind*, identifies this type of thinking as *dualistic thinking*, which is the ability to uncover and resolve contradictions in opposing and seemingly incompatible views.

Boomers at age 50, 60 and beyond are much more likely to accept and process ideas, messages, and communications from companies and organizations that make Conditional claims. Claims that leave room for interpretation will more likely be interpreted. Claims that don't will likely be ignored.

A recent ad for a financial services firm had the headline, "Introducing the biggest change to the 401(k) since, *well*, the 401(k)." Cute headline, but one that immediately sets off a red flag in Boomer Consumers and makes them wonder, "says who?" Claims about the biggest, most important, best, only and other absolute statements will likely be met with skepticism and doubt by most Boomer Consumers. Once more, marketers tend to forget that Boomers are the most experienced consumers of advertising today in America. They literally have seen it all, countless times.

A more effective approach, then, is to be honest and straightforward in what you say about your product and service, without exaggeration or absolute claims. Make statements that are true and accurate. Also, stay away from even using comparative claims. Just talk about your attributes and benefits on their own merit. Most Boomers know that any comparison against a competitor will result in your coming out on top, because only certain conditions are used. Once more, those kinds of claims are just no longer believable to Boomer Consumers, who have seen it all.

Keanu Reeves :: Paul Reiser :: Jean Reno :: Paul "Pee-Wee Herman" Reubens :: Ving Rhames :: Michael

Conditional claims are more effective. Words like "if" and "when" and "for people like this" and other qualifiers can enable you to make believable statements. Here are some examples:

- *If you're nearing retirement and looking for investment strategies that make sense for you now, call us today.* Not "everybody" and not "the best investments" or any other claim, just a statement about the services you offer.

- *People who come to our fitness center feel fit, healthy, and empowered.* Again, a statement, not a comparative claim. It doesn't mean that you, the reader, will come and feel fit, healthy and empowered. But you might.

- *Our community is filled with those who can choose to live anywhere.* This provocative statement suggests important differences in this community, but doesn't actually make any comparative claims. And once more, it is about the people who want to live there more so than the community itself.

Crafting messages to connect with older Boomers requires careful attention to language and approach. Today's Boomers have a lifetime of experiences with bad, false, or misleading advertising.

Summary

Marketing to today's Boomer Consumer has a much better chance of success if you use Conditional positioning and language. For example, the sentence, *"Boomers reject black and white claims as unbelievable"* strains credibility because it is an absolute claim. The sentence, *"Most Boomers prefer claims that are conditional"* is more believable because it has words like "most" and "prefer."

- Rational, absolute claims or product positions, from the perspective of the company or organization, are not as successful with today's Boomer Consumers. Emotional, conditional claims from the perspective of the consumer are much more effective.

Richards :: Natasha Richardson :: Patricia Richardson :: Alan Rickman :: Eric Roberts :: Tim Robins :: Howard

- Stay away from "best," "only" and other superlative claims. Instead talk about your attributes and benefits without comparative claims or use conditional phrases: "If this is your situation, then…" or "if you are like this person, then…" or "people in this life stage often…"

Rush :: Kurt Russell :: Rene Russo :: Meg Ryan :: Bob Saget :: Susan Sarandon :: Jennifer Saunders :: Peter

Chapter 13
Rule 9: Use Life Stage, Not Age

*A*t 52 years old, Al Harwood has spent most of his career in financial services, working for six different firms over the last 30 years. Today he's quite successful, serving as a divisional vice president for a multibillion dollar insurance company. Divorced and recently remarried, he's the father of three: a 22-year-old daughter, a 20-year-old son and brand-new baby girl. His own father was an electrician and died of a heart attack at age 58. His mother lives nearby. She's 82 herself and healthy, but Al spends a fair amount of time with her, making sure she's doing okay. Right now he would describe himself as a caregiver towards her emotional well-being, although not her physical health. Not yet anyway....

Al has paid for two college educations and has started putting money away for a third, set to start in 2024, when he is 70. Al works out three times a week, plays golf, and travels for his job frequently. He owns a TiVo, iPod, and HDTV.

When it comes to media consumption, Al is like many of his Boomer contemporaries who are empty nesters or caregivers for their parents. But then again, he's not, thanks to his new daughter. He's like any new dad with a baby. Al may not be a typical Boomer at midlife; is there even such a thing?

Introduction: The Multiple Life Stages of Boomers

In Chapter 3 we gave an overview of the sociological aspects of today's Boomer Consumer and focused on the different life stage and life styles of this generation of 78 million. In this chapter we're going to explore the use of Life Stages as an effective way to connect with Boomers today.

As mentioned in Chapter 3, for decades marketers relied upon age as a key indicator of the life stage of a consumer. Someone's age revealed much about where they were on life's path, and therefore, what products or services would be relevant to them. With Boomers now in their 40's, 50's and entering their 60's, it is much more difficult, if not impossible, to use age as the key indicator of life stage. That's because Boomers have been living cyclical, rather than linear lives. They have gone to college or gotten educated at times other than in their late teens and early 20's. They married, started a family, then divorced, then re-married and started another family years later. They have had more than one career. They have lived in more than one market. They are caring for older parents or relatives, or they are raising young children, or both.

In a national study, we asked Boomers to describe where they were in life right now. One is four say they are "retired," but one in six say they are in a "new job." Only 50% label themselves "parent" but 73% are "empty nesters" – meaning the children have left the house (aren't they still parents even if the kid isn't home?).

Today, it's hard to connect with Boomer Consumers simply by knowing their age. You have to know and understand their life stage. Marketers and advertisers can take advantage of this, helping them identify with consumers at a similar place in life. In "TV Land's" landmark study of Boomers done by *Age Wave's* Dr. Ken Dychtwald, one key finding was that the vast majority of Boomers were uninterested in products or services that featured people or situations they could not relate to. "If it isn't about me, then it isn't for me" seems to be Boomer logic.

Life Stages of Today's Boomer

From our work with BIGresearch and their national monthly surveys of 7,000 consumers, called the Consumer Intentions & Actions survey, we can quantify certain life stages of Boomers, which can help you effectively reach them. Here are the biggest groups, from the smallest to the largest.

Boomers with Kids in College

According to the U.S. Census, as of October 2005, about 10.8 million people ages 18-24 are enrolled in two-year, four-year and graduate programs. The vast majority of those young adults have parents who are Boomers.

Wesley Snipes :: Suzanne Somers :: Sissy Spacek :: Kevin Spacey :: James Spader :: Sylvester Stallone ::

The BIGresearch data also tells us that about 1 in 20 Boomers, or about 4 million, will have a child starting college in the next six months. Given this, we're not surprised by the increasing number of marketers showing people in ads with college-aged children, like the Lowe's Home Improvement commercial mentioned in earlier chapters with the young man coming home to do his laundry. While not all Boomers have kids in college right now, the majority of them either have had one or more children enrolled in higher education or will be dealing with the situation in the next 5-10 years.

Boomers with Teenagers

In the spring of 2007, 30 million Boomers still have children at home under the age of 18. The majority of them are teenagers or will be within a very few years. That explains a recent print ad from Charles Schwab, the financial services firm, with a headline that says, "I have a teenager. I don't need a broker who doesn't listen to me." The obvious target for this message is Boomers with teenagers, and/or consumers in their 40's. The ad doesn't scream out "Hey you, Boomers," but reaches them by targeting parents of teenagers.

Boomer Grandparents

The largest and most lasting life stage Boomers are entering is that of grandparenthood. In fact, we think grandparent-oriented marketing will be the most popular and effective way to get the attention of Boomers Consumers in the coming years. And being a grandparent doesn't equate itself with "old;" the average age of a new, first time grandparent today is 47, according to *Grand* Magazine. In our work with BIGresearch we found that, as of spring 2007, about 28 million Boomers are already grandparents, with 4,000 more joining their ranks every day. One thing that hasn't changed with generations that also applies to Boomers : Once a grandparent, always a grandparent.

BoomBox

Facts & Figures on Baby Boomer Grandparents

- Of the 78 million Boomers, 35% are already grandparents — some 27.2 million.

- Of all grandparents in the United States today, 58% are Boomers.

- The average age of a Boomer grandparent today is 53.2 years old.

- Only 12% of Boomer Grandparents are retired. That suggests they have money to spend on their grandkids that older, retired grandparents don't have.

- Being a Boomer Grandparent has an impact on shopping and spending patterns:

  - Boomer Grandparents are twice as likely to shop discount stores for children's clothes as Boomers who aren't grandparents.

  - Boomer Grandparents are 46% more likely to shop department stores for children's clothes as Boomers who aren't grandparents.

  - In an average month, Boomer Grandparents say they spend 35% more on children's clothes than Boomers who aren't grandparents. And they spend 54% more than older grandparents (born before 1946) do.

  - When asked their plans for the next 90 days, Boomer Grandparents are twice as likely to say they'll be spending more on toys than they did at this time last year, and 1.5 times more likely to say they'll spend more on children's clothes, as compared to Boomers who aren't grandparents.

Patrick Swayze :: Philip Michael Thomas :: Richard Thomas :: Emma Thompson :: Lea Thompson :: Billy Bob

- Even when it comes to car purchases, being a grandparent changes motivations. When asked what motivated them to buy their last car, about 15% of Boomer Grandparents say they "needed more room" while only 4% of Boomers who aren't grandparents gave that reason.

- Boomer Grandparents are 23% more likely to say that over the last six months they are "spending more time with their family" than Boomers who aren't grandparents.

Source: Boomer Project analysis of BIGresearch CIA Study, February 2007

Single Boomers

While not necessarily a life stage, single, never married Boomers comprise a surprising 13%. Divorced and separated Boomers are another 16%. Widowed Boomers are another 3%. Added together, Boomers living the single life make up one third of the cohort, forever proving that the "traditional" family of Dad, Mom, and two kids is a thing of the past.

This huge segment of Boomers has been largely ignored by marketers. Every once in a while we'll run across a commercial with a single Mom (such as the Home Depot commercial in Chapter 9) or Dad, but it is rare. But most of the time marketers show traditional families. We anticipate this will change, slowly, over the next several years as more and more marketers better understand the household composition of their consumers.

Thornton :: Jennifer Tilly :: Meg Tilly :: Marisa Tomei :: John Travolta :: Kathleen Turner :: Lindsay Wagner ::

 **Boom**Box

Mining the Single Life

Does living single mean being alone? Not necessarily, even in single person households. In fact, even among Divorced Boomer households, 49% have two or more people living in the home, with an average household of 1.93 people. Married Boomer households include 2.97 people on average.

Despite the smaller household size, Divorced Boomers outspend Married Boomers monthly at the grocery store by about 7% per person. In other categories, like monthly expenses on entertainment or clothing, the per-person difference is even larger. Of course, single Boomer households do report lower income levels, since there is typically only one income, and they do tend to be more conservative about their spending plans, focusing more on satisfying their needs than their wants.

Still, marketers who ignore single Boomers risk chasing away perhaps their most lucrative customers — ones with money to spend and an even greater willingness to spend it. So make sure to keep single, divorced, and widowed Boomers in mind when developing promotional materials and even portion sizes. And while you're at it, think about showing an empty nester Boomer who is a single parent. Plenty are out there.

Caregivers

Another Life Stage many Boomers, especially Boomer women, find themselves in now is caregiver for their elderly parents or relatives. It is a stage of life that often comes about quickly, as the result of a medical condition or emergency, and can last from several days, to weeks, to months and years. While it is important for all marketers to understand

Lesley Ann Warren :: Denzel Washington :: Damon Wayans :: Keenan Ivory Wayans :: Sigourney Weaver ::

this life stage and its impact on today's Boomer Consumer, it does not typically offer much of an inroad in terms of reaching and connecting with Boomers, other than to demonstrate empathy and understanding.

Unless you have a product or service specifically related to helping Boomers or their elderly parents as part of the caregiving life stage, our advice is to steer clear of marketing to this segment. If you do need to target Boomers in this situation, do so carefully and mindful that it is a stress-filled topic.

Casting for Boomers

Showing Boomer life stages in marketing materials should be done with caution. First, *be careful what you call Boomers*. Boomers don't respond well to labels, even the term "Boomer" has drawbacks in advertising and marketing. Older Boomers also reject any term suggesting age or implying that they are indeed old. They can't stand traditional terms like "senior" and "mature adult," as covered earlier. "Grandmother" or "granddad" also has image problems, as Boomers are not embracing those exact terms for themselves. Instead, pet names like "Mimi" and "Pop-pop" are gaining in favor, or even more personalized versions.

Clever marketers can work around this limitation by simply showing a Boomer grandparent in a situation with a grandchild, and not labeling either, or only labeling the grandchild. MasterCard has run a print ad with a young boy identified as a "grandson" without actually showing any grandparents. Such an approach is good because Boomer grandparents can put themselves in the picture, and MasterCard has solved the problem of casting the right age and look for the grandparent.

A hotel chain did the same with a magazine ad targeting "Empty Nesters." They show two unoccupied Adirondack chairs on a dock overlooking a pristine lake. Overlaid on top of the visual are two Web site pull-down menus. In the first menu the selection is "Adults: 2" and the second is "Children: Off to college, finally." Nowhere in the ad is the term "empty nester" used, but clearly that is the target. Using the two empty chairs also solves the problem of casting the right models.

Forest Whitaker :: Dianne Wiest :: Cindy Williams :: Robin Williams :: Vanessa Williams :: Bruce Willis ::

That leads to our second caution: *Be careful with casting*. Whether it is for a brochure or a TV commercial, trying to find someone the right age with the right look to portray a 50-something Boomer is tricky. Remember, a typical 54-year-old Boomer sees themselves as 14 years younger than they are – or about 40. On the other hand, the typical designer or art director working in ad agencies and marketing departments is probably in their late 20's or early 30's. Their impression of what a 50-something might look like is considerably different than a Boomer's self image.

To make this point, we often show a picture of actor Pierce Brosnan, age 52 and a recent "Bond. James Bond," during our seminars. He is a grandfather two times over, yet hardly personifies the usual representation of "Gramps" on TV or in print ads.

Our advice to marketers is to cast talent that looks about ten years younger than the age of your intended audience, and then to put them in situations typical of the target age. For example, in the Lowe's Home Improvement commercial with the college-aged son bringing home laundry, both the actors playing Mom and Dad look like they are 40-45. Most Boomers put off having children until they were older, so it is more likely that a Boomer with a 20-year-old would be around 50 or even older. Casting younger-looking talent and putting them in situations most 50-year-olds find themselves in works with today's Boomer Consumer. Put the same talent in a commercial with young children in diapers, and they'll be seen as younger parents. Boomers with their youthful self-perception will believe what they see in their mind's eye more readily than what is on the screen (and sadly sometimes in the mirror). So rather than perceiving the product as being for someone "old," they will better be able to relate to it.

Far too often marketers err on the other side of age when it comes to casting someone to portray a Boomer. Marketers tend to think that since the first Boomers are now entering their 60's, all Boomers are that age. In truth, the median age of the 78 million Boomers is just now 50. And those 50-year-olds think they are not yet 40.

Debra Winger :: James Woods :: Jean Claude Van Damme :: Barry Van Dyke :: Chow Yun-Fat :: Ian Ziering ::

When it comes to casting for Boomers, it's better to err on the side of youth than old age.

Life Style and Attitude Marketing

As also mentioned in Chapter 3, another effective way to target and reach today's Boomer Consumer is by using Life Style marketing. Positioning your product or service along life style dimensions allows for appeal across all age groups. There are several options, and you can:

- Show Boomers who live healthy, physically fit lives to appeal to Boomers who see themselves that way.

- Show Boomers in urban settings, grabbing life by the horns, to appeal to Boomers who feel they have the same approach.

- Show Boomers in a community setting, volunteering or mentoring, to appeal to that life style and attitude.

Any of those approaches is ageless. It doesn't matter how old you are; if you are this kind of person, then this product or service is right for you.

A related approach is to position your product or service on an attitudinal dimension. For years Harley-Davidson effectively marketed their motorcycles as perfect for someone with a rebellious attitude and love for freedom of the road. Most of the time the rider on the motorcycle is wearing a helmet, making it impossible to gauge their age. That was done intentionally because Harley-Davidson doesn't care about the age of their buyer, just their attitude.

Disney markets the same way and focuses on people who enjoy and want the fantasyland experience. They really don't care about age, just attitude, and their ads reflect this.

There are as many attitudes that cut across age as life styles, making it an especially effective approach to reach both Boomers and younger consumers.

Target Older and Reach Young

We've also uncovered what we call "The OC Rule," with "OC" meaning "Older Consumer" of course. The rule is this: "Products, services, and even advertising, designed for older consumers can also appeal to younger consumers. The opposite is not so true."

Case in point: Do you own Oxo Brand "Good Grips" kitchen utensils? In millions of homes the answer is "yes." But do you also have arthritis? Good Grips were designed for older consumers with arthritic hands. Consumers of any age have embraced Good Grips because they are easier to hold and use in the kitchen, no matter what the condition of your hands. Designers call it "universal design," meaning the product can be used by anyone, regardless of disability or handicap.

At the other end of the spectrum, how many of you have Red Bull energy drinks in your fridge? If you're older than 40, we would guess you don't. Red Bull is for younger consumers and marketed to them, and not at all appealing to older consumers.

Our advice to marketers is to think about the OC Rule when developing products, services, and marketing messages. Focusing exclusively on the young will deliver that audience to you, but only that audience. Focus on Older Consumers and you may attract everyone.

Summary

Boomers will respond to messages applicable to them and their lives right now. The best way to connect with them is to use messages related to certain relevant Life Stages. These include:

- Boomers with teenagers
- Boomers with college-aged kids
- Boomers with empty nests
- Boomers who are now grandparents
- Boomers who are single
- Boomers who are caregivers

Tracy Austin :: Alan Autry :: Charles Barkley :: Johnny Bench :: Larry Bird :: Bonnie Blair :: Brian Boitano ::

Another approach is to target Boomers by their life style or by their attitudes.

Be careful what you call Boomers, avoiding as many labels as you can. Let them fill in their own labels. Also, when casting actors and models to portray Boomers in your marketing materials, err on the side of using younger-looking talent and put them in age-appropriate situations that fit the needs of your Boomer audience.

Chapter 14
Rule 10:
Learn Baby, Learn

In 2006, Home Instead Senior Care, an Omaha-based company that franchises businesses to provide non-medical in-home companion care to older consumers, conducted a national study among Boomers with living parents. The Boomer Project was brought in to help Home Instead interpret the data and uncover implications for their marketing efforts.

Although the research findings are confidential, we can say that Boomers as caregivers and supervisors of caregivers for their parents are finding themselves in uncharted territory. Despite being at the peak of their careers and earning their highest salary levels, they are wholly unprepared for this role. Most everything encountered at this stage is new and sometimes frightening. But the interesting thing is that those who have been through it are at a different place now than those who haven't. Experience is a great teacher even if a sorrowful one in this case.

So it's a good thing Home Instead conducted this research. As you'll see in this chapter, what you learn from today's Boomer Consumer will likely be different tomorrow.

Introduction: Delving Into the Boomer Psyche

Interest in understanding the Boomer market is at an all-time high. More and more C-class executives (CEO's, CFO's, CMO's) and their boards are coming to the irrefutable conclusion that the biggest opportunity for growth over the next 20 years will come from the very group that made the 18-49 segment so desirable in the last 40 years.

We're delighted that so many people are now finally "getting it." While we're focusing on the "how" aspect of marketing to Boomers, we've done our fair share of evangelizing on the "why" to corporate and non-profit America, and beyond. In addition to Home Instead, we've helped major U.S. organizations like Pfizer Consumer Health Care, Hershey's, Genworth Financial, Media General, Samsung, SunTrust, American Heart Association and many others understand their Boomer-related opportunities. We've even worked with the real estate development community in Panama, helping them figure out how they could attract

"Dr. J" Erving :: Chris Evert :: Patrick Ewing :: Lou Ferrigno :: Rollie Fingers :: Carlton Fisk :: Peggy Fleming ::

U.S. Baby Boomers to invest, retire, or move there. Just let us know if you're interested in information on upscale condos overlooking a certain scenic canal-like waterway in Panama.

The overarching perspective is this – you can't just take a snapshot in time or conduct one study and hope to understand everything about today's Boomer Consumer. The Boomer Consumer is a moving target and you need to keep moving along with them. And the best way to do this is to first learn everything you can about Boomers, from climbing on the shoulders of Boomer experts like us and getting the "big picture" and then constantly studying Boomer behavior in such a manner that it relates to your specific business. You can jump-start the process by tapping into the resources outlined in this chapter.

Boomer Required Reading

If you have benefited from this book, you can learn more from the following "general" generational and "marketing" generational books:

- *Age Wave*, Dr. Ken Dychtwald. Ken is one of, if not the first, to wake up to the power of the Boomer generation as relates to the American economy. This book is a good place to orient to the importance of the Boomer generation. Ken also produced and narrated *Boomer Century*, a 2007 documentary that aired on PBS. Visit www.agewave.com or boomercentury.com for more information.

- *Ageless Marketing*, David Wolfe. We've mentioned David's work in several places in our book. David's first book on the topic of the changing demographic landscape for marketers was published in 1989, when the first Boomers were just 43 years old. The 2004 version of *Ageless Marketing* builds on David's thinking and outlines reasons why today's Boomers behave the way they do. It is a deep, thoughtful, and careful examination of how to market to Boomer Consumers. Also check out agelessmarketing. typepad.com for additional information.

George Foreman :: Steve Garvey :: Dwight Gooden :: Wayne Gretzky :: Tony Gwynn :: "Marvelous" Marvin

- *Prime Time Women*, Marti Barletta. Marti is a long-time expert on the power and importance of women consumers, and in this book focuses on women in their 50's, 60's and beyond. It's another great resource with practical tips and techniques.

- *Marketing to Leading Edge Boomers*, Brent Green. Brent is a direct marketing expert who wants to rid the modern world of "ageism" and what he calls "genism" (generational bias). He's working to change Boomers' reputation - left over from the 1960s, 70s, and 80s - from hippies and self-absorbed yuppies. His book discusses why today's Boomers deserve more careful consideration in marketing. Brent can also be found at marketingtoboomers.com.

- *Advertising to Boomers*, Chuck Nyren. A "how to" book from a former advertising executive who is part visionary and part curmudgeon. Chuck's premise is that older Boomer copywriters and art directors could develop advertising that works with today's Boomers, but no agency will hire them because they are too old. He's discusses it in great detail on his blog, advertisingtobabyboomers. blogspot.com.

- *The Fourth Turning*, William Strauss and Neil Howe. Not a marketing book per se but a look at the cycles of history and four re-occurring generational archetypes. The book offers up proof of the observation by Winston Churchill: "Those who don't study history are doomed to repeat it."

Review Existing Boomer Research Studies

As the media celebrated the 60th birthdays of popular Boomers starting in 2006, study after study has been released that not only profiles and segments Boomers, but also paints a picture of where they are headed and what they will do with the rest of their lives. The best sources include AARP (www.aarp.org) and MetLife (www.metlife.com), while others may be less trustworthy. Most studies are posted online by their sponsors and are available for your review. Read them with caution because many were originally conducted and promoted to advance their sponsors' interests.

Hagler :: Dorothy Hamill :: Scott Hamilton :: Ricky Henderson :: Hulk Hogan :: Evander Holyfield :: Bo Jackson

We also collect and catalog the best free information we find and post it at the Boomer Project's site: www.boomerproject.com.

Reviewing these "free" studies is a sensible and worthwhile step in understanding the Boomer Consumer. But just keep in mind who sponsored them.

Conduct Your Own Proprietary Research Studies

There no better way to understand the Boomer Consumer than to conduct your own primary research. When you do, it's an excellent way to learn something new and insightful that will help drive your business. However, it should deliver relevant and meaningful insights and actionable next steps that will help you get inside the mind of today's Boomer Consumers as well as their wallets.

Through our partner firm, SIR Research, we have "real world" experiences from which we have learned subtle nuances about effective research design and interpretation when it comes to older populations – important considerations to take into account when studying today's Boomer Consumer. They include the following suggestions which can help you implement your own study.

Insights often come from generational differences

When we see statistics reported from a study in the media, our immediate response is akin to the classic line from the Robot in the mid-1960s CBS-TV series *Lost in Space*. A favorite of Boomer kids everywhere, he waves his slinky-like arms, shouting, "Danger Will Robinson! Danger!"

That's because a finding or statistic, simply stated on its own and absent from any comparison, may not be all that revealing. In fact, all it could reveal is what the study sponsor wants to it to reveal: "37% of Boomers like spear fishing, reported the spear fishing trade association on Monday."

What does that really tell you? Do more than one third of Boomers like to go spear fishing, or do they just say they like it in general? Is that more or less than Generation X consumers? How about the Silent generation at the same age? Did they like spear fishing more than that? At the end of the day, as we've heard from our research director, "a number, in and of itself, is meaningless."

However, when a data point is shown in comparison to other data points, the finding and related insight likely comes from the data itself. We believe meaningful research-inspired insights come from understanding differences and similarities – how one number compares to another. That's why our generational research doesn't just cover Boomers, it usually includes respondents from the four living adult generations: Silent, Boomers, Gen X, and Gen Y (a.k.a. Millennials or Echo Boomers). Many of the self-proclaimed studies focus exclusively on Boomers. How can they say Boomers are different if they don't show the comparison to other age cohorts?

In gathering responses across multiple generations, we simply ask what year were you born and then later sort the data based on commonly accepted generational definitions – that is, *Boomers 1946-64*. Actually, it is beyond frustrating that most studies, even from the Bureau of Statistics in the Department of Labor, just ask respondents to identify their age within standard ten-year age breaks (18-24, 25-34, 35-44, 45-54, 55-64, 65+). The section, "What a Difference a Day Makes" in Chapter 3 discusses how limiting that approach is.

Expect a built-in positive response bias

When conducting research among today's older Boomers, think positive! As covered in Chapter 7, advertisers trying to appeal to older consumers need to use positive, emotionally meaningful imagery. Craft messages from the standpoint of possibilities, not a recapitulation of how bad the future could be if you fail to do this or that.

You will likely get a disproportionately higher number of positive responses from older adults than from younger ones on the same questions or issues. Conversely, you'll also get fewer negative responses from older consumers, who simply can't or won't dwell on the negative. Consider these factors while probing for insights and formulating research-inspired action steps.

Some practical study design issues may come into play. While it is not always possible to avoid negative words or topics in a questionnaire, try to phrase questions in the positive if you want the full attention of older Boomers. This includes avoiding research questions that approach issues from a negative angle ("Which of the following is the least attractive option in a new car?") or the use of negative agreement questions ("Which of the following statements accurately reflects your point of view: 'I don't like leather seats.' 'I don't use my tilt steering wheel.' 'I don't know what anti-lock brakes are.'").

Responses often come in shades of gray.

As Chapter 12 discussed, older Boomers see shades of gray more so than blacks or whites. Researchers at SIR have experienced this themselves through the more than one million consumer interviews conducted over the past 43 years. In study after study, SIR found that older consumers feel that many of their answers need further explanation. They aren't comfortable being forced into absolutes, even on a scale. "Don't knows" are easier to give as an answer.

This is most notable in the thousands of physician-related health care studies SIR has conducted. Young doctors are quick to provide yes-or-no, black-or-white answers to many research questions. Older doctors, on the other hand, are not so swift to judge. They usually begin their answers with, "It depends."

Simply put, questions presented as absolutes - "all or nothing" - may not resonate with Boomer Consumers. Research shouldn't force people into a researcher's world, but rather get people to explain their world. Fortunately, more and more researchers have embraced this philosophical perspective. So, if at all possible, avoid "black and white" research.

In surveys targeting older respondents, we provide them with ways to add "other" to attribute lists or add explanations as to why they answered the way they did. Often this is done through clearly stated optional open-ended questions that start with, "Please elaborate or comment." While we do not always collect the information from all of these extra questions, we have found respondents appreciate them and use them often. And we often gain further insight into the related issue.

Always explore emotional and rational perspectives

In Chapter 6 we talked about the need to use emotionally meaningful concepts, words, and images to better connect with today's Boomer Consumer. That applies to research design as well.

Effective research targeting older consumers must probe emotional responses – what's happening and why. This causes problems for marketing researchers because emotions are spontaneous and practically impossible to explain or discuss in a research setting. They just erupt from within at the point of purchase or some other point – and oftentimes are even subconscious, making it impossible to capture at all.

Needless to say, it is beyond difficult to study emotional responses through most traditional research approaches. Consumers rarely act in a laboratory setting they way they do in real life. So when it comes to probing emotions, our researchers shun survey statistics in favor of qualitative research - passive anthropological observation and one-on-one open-ended questioning. We observe consumers at home, work, play, and in the malls and around store aisles. The data are our observations. The objective is to learn and catalog an array of behavior and the "in the moment" feelings. We view the research participants as the teacher. As the student, we are there to simply learn from them – why they do the things they do, why they go to certain places, and the reasons behind their purchasing decisions. How does it make them feel?

The key is to totally detach your own ideas about the product or service being studied – to immerse yourself in how the "teacher" sees the world.

Mark McGwire :: Mark Messier :: Joe Montana :: Eddie Murray :: Martina Navratilova :: Greg Norman ::

Take into account the physical aspects of growing older

Age affects vision, hearing, feeling sensations, and cognitive and motor abilities. This, in turn, has an impact on a person's social skills and ability to participate in research.

When designing any research to be used with older consumers, field test it with them. Make sure they can see, hear, understand, and interact with it; and overall "get it." You and your research team may know what you're asking, but older consumers don't process information the same way, especially if you are 20 or more years younger. So test the survey instrument in advance. It will help gauge its effectiveness.

BoomBox

Five Boomer Research Design Tips

After 43 years of interviewing GIs and now the Silent generation cohorts as they defined America's aging consumer market, we can say with confidence that insightful and actionable research among Boomer Consumers requires a thoughtful approach to research design — how a study is conducted. Whether it's one-on-one interviewing, focus groups, or survey research, the following basic practices should help you get the most out of your research investigations.

1. **Respect everyone's time.** Older consumers want to be treated in a dignified manner. This is especially important when it comes to Boomers. To their way of thinking, the world has always revolved around them. They don't expect it to stop just because they're older. In fact, our research suggests that they expect respect and attention now more than ever because they've "earned it." But they also feel showing respect and giving focused attention is falling short. No surprise that Boomers' expectations for customer service are higher than younger counterparts, two generations

Hakeem Olajuwon :: Robert Parish :: William "Refrigerator" Perry :: Jerry Rice :: Cathy Rigby :: Cal Ripken ::

that have grown up in a much more casual self-service. Thoughtful and considerate "customer appreciation phases" like, "Is this a convenient time?" go a long way. This will become more important with the advent and growth of research as it relates to Boomer Consumers.

2. **Provide detailed directions.** Take the time to fully explain survey research instructions and provide helpful markers along the way. This starts with the initial setup. There is always the tendency to tell potential respondents the estimated minimum time required to take a survey. Rarely do we offer a maximum time. You're better off telling them exactly how long is required or providing a range – "Most people complete this survey in 10-12 minutes, but you may take longer if you wish.

By providing more detailed explanations and offering markers along the way, respondents clearly understand what you are looking for and can tell how far they've gone or how far they have to go in the research process. Sentences like, "These next five questions will...." are very helpful, too. For each different type of question (i.e., rating scale, lists, etc.), use clear and precise instructions, such as, "Select only one from the following list" rather than "Select one." Encourage the older consumer to keep participating by expressions of gratitude - "We appreciate your time so far, just a few more questions concerning xyz ..."

3. **Be there for them.** Make it easy for them to get help if they get stuck or become confused by explicitly stating, "Just ask if you have any questions about this survey" for telephone or in-person interviews. Include an email hyperlink on every page of a Web survey or a phone number on every page of a printed survey. Make sure you're always available to answer questions.

4. **Make it personal.** All questions and comments should be asked or written from the perspective of the respondent – "you" and not from the perspective of the research sponsor or researcher – "we" or "us." Older consumers want their opinions heard and are willing respondents. But if the questions are not about them personally, they lose interest. For example, do not simply have declarative statements as questions: "Rate the following companies in terms of customer friendliness." Instead, use polite respondent-focused language like: "Please tell us how you rate each of the following companies in terms of customer friendliness." The same goes for agreement questions. Use first-person pronouns such as "I agree with this statement" and "This applies to me," versus the second-person pronoun "You."

5. **Be careful what you call study participants: Our Boomer Project research has tested age-based labels for ads and articles across many industries.** The results suggest a lack of consensus on the ideal label. Not surprisingly, however, we found that 98% of Boomers don't want to be called "seniors." Who's going to call Bruce Springsteen, Christy Brinkley, or Kim Basinger "senior?" But terms like older adult, middle age, and active adult fell flat, too. As pointed out earlier, 68% of the Boomers we surveyed even disliked the label "Baby Boomer." Their preference, like most Silent generation members, was not to be labeled at all. With an appreciation of how Baby Boomers look at their own age, it makes sense that they would shun any traditional labels relating to it. The implication for research is to avoid using wording like, "Compared to other (seniors, Boomers, elders, etc.) would you say you are more likely…" Just say, "Compared to people like you…."

Doing Your Own

There are many ways to design proprietary research targeting today's Boomer Consumers, but that is another book altogether. To get the best research outcome – actionable insights, take into account that today's Boomers are older, wiser, and different than younger adults. Plan and conduct your studies accordingly.

Which leads us to the most important point in understanding the Boomer Consumer – they are constantly evolving. One study is only a snapshot in time. To become a real expert on the Boomer Consumer you need to embrace a "continuous learning" perspective. And a good place to start after you finish the next chapter is our Web site, www. boomerconsumer.com

Visit boomerconsumer.com

OK, it's time for a commercial break, but one that should help with your marketing efforts. The Web site that accompanies this book, www. boomerconsumer.com, contains articles, studies, books, contacts, and even suggestions on how to market to today's Boomer Consumer. We continuously update this repository of marketing treasures, so make it a regular surfing haunt. Better yet, sign up for email updates when we post new studies or for our free monthly newsletter, *Jumpin' Jack Flash*. If you like that, consider our paid monthly newsletter, *BoomerMarketingNews*. You can download a past issue from www.boomerproject.com.

Summary

Today's Boomer Consumer is a moving target. The first Boomers began turning 60 in 2006 and will keep doing so for the next 17 years. How they feel today about any one topic or any one product category will change and evolve just as it always has. And knowing how they feel today won't tell you what they'll want in five years. No one knows exactly how 78 million older Boomers will change our and their lives. What we do know is that they will continue to have a profound impact on our society and economy.

To truly understand the Boomer market, you need to keep moving with it. And the best way to do that is to become a continuous learner – *learn, baby learn!* Start by first understanding the body of knowledge created by the early "Boomer industry" thought leaders like Ken Dychtwald, David Wolfe, and others. Then examine the more celebrated studies and the real experts on Boomers - Boomers themselves – through your own proprietary research. Observe, listen, and learn where Boomers are in their lives and where and how your product or service can serve their evolving needs. And tap into your Boomer Consumer resource center – www.boomerconsumer.com.

Letterman :: Bill Maher :: Dr. Phil (McGraw) :: Dr. Drew Pinsky :: Robin Quivers :: Pat Sajak :: Marc Summers

Part 3
What Next?

Part 3: Introduction

When we work with clients around the country, or give seminars and workshops, we're often asked about where Boomers are going. What will drive their consuming behavior in the future?

We think that question offers us the best place to end this book on today's Boomer Consumer. This final chapter explores what might be next for Boomers as they grow older. Will they pursue the fountain of youth, trying to maintain a Peter Pan-like approach until their dying breath? Or will they come together like during the 1960s and solve the significant issues of our time? "The next ten years are going to be very defining for America," said David Gergen, professor of public service at Harvard's John F. Kennedy School of Government and former White House adviser to Presidents Nixon, Ford, Reagan, and Clinton, on Ken Dychtwald's PBS documentary *Boomer Century*. "The big question about the Baby Boom generation is, is it going to grow up in time and get serious about facing up to the challenges that are going to be here for our children and grandchildren, or are we going to slide by and leave them with a really big mess?"

We're pretty sure Boomers will get serious. There really isn't any choice.

Boomer Musicians: Paula Abdul :: Bryan Adams :: Duane Allman :: Gregg Allman :: Tori Amos :: Ian An-

Chapter 15
The "Golden" Rule

Gordon Walker, 60, is the CEO of JABA, the regional area agency on aging in Charlottesville, Virginia. Framed on his wall is an original poster promoting three days of music, peace, and love. The place: Woodstock. The year: 1969. Gordon was in California at the time but was there in spirit.

In the early 1970s he found himself serving as a young staffer for a junior Senator assigned to the Special Committee on Aging. That's when he first got interested in older Americans. By the time he got his ear pierced at age 36, he had committed himself to working in the aging field, trying to make sure older people got the services they needed and the respect they deserved.

Today Gordon sees a never-before confluence of events – Boomers reaching their time on life's stage for the last act, a time when many will start thinking about their legacy to their community, their fellow citizens, and the planet. This will take place during the heyday of the longevity revolution, suggesting Boomers will live longer than any previous generation. Yet it will also happen right as Social Security, Medicare, and Medicaid start to run dry. Gordon calls it a "Perfect Storm," and he hopes, unlike the book and movie with that name, it ends well for everyone.

He's doing his part to make sure it does, as you'll discover later in the chapter. Will other Boomers?

Introduction: Boomers and Mortality

Boomers at midlife are actually, and actuarially, past life's midpoint. Statistically, a Boomer reaching age 60 should live to an average of 82.5, according to insurance industry figures. AARP did a study among Boomers at 50 and asked them how long they thought they'd live. On average, the response was 35 more years.

Even if a Boomer at 50 is off by ten years and they live to 95, they are still past the halfway point at 50. Given that, we aren't surprised when we find most Boomers over 50 have come to accept the reality that we're all terminal. That doesn't mean they are ready to hang it up, but they will acknowledge they won't live forever. And it also means they are not pursuing the Fountain of Youth. Despite being the most recent generation credited with making America a youth-obsessed culture — the same thing happened back in the 1920s with the Flappers and F. Scott Fitzgerald's contemporaries — Boomers themselves have stopped being youth-obsessed and are likely going to embrace old age and growing older unlike any generation before them.

In fact, Boomers may actually make being old "cool." But more on that later.

Viva the Vital!

The pursuit, from age 50-90, we predict won't be for the Fountain of Youth but the Fountain of Vitality. Boomers will spend time, money, and energy trying to maintain their vitality until the day they die. *Viva the Vital!*— Long live the vital! — will be the mantra.

Our prediction is based in large part on the Boomer generation archetype: driven, transformational, and "self" centered. Boomers at every stage of life have looked at how their parents, or other earlier generations, did things and decided essentially that it wasn't going to work for them.

Take, for example, how Boomer women reacted to having babies. They saw how their mothers had done it, trusting blindly in their doctors and following the traditional rules and regulations that kept husbands out of the delivery room and away from the entire process. Instead, Boomer women decide to reinvent the wheel so to speak, not only learning all they could about birthing and being proactive in choosing their doctors but involving their husbands as well. Husbands went to the doctor's appointments, attended birthing classes where they trained as coaches, and were present in the delivery room, even cutting the cord. Boomer women affected a permanent change in the way all women give birth.

Boomers have already decided to develop a new approach to "retirement" and this next stage of life, even if they haven't quite figured out all the details. They are confident that it won't be spent on some front porch whittling and whistling in a rocking chair. Or sitting by passively and waiting for the children and grandchildren to visit.

Buckingham :: Jimmy Buffett :: Dewey Bunnell :: Kate Bush :: David Byrne :: Irene Cara :: Kim Carnes :: John

One driver of this need to change is the self-realization that the AARP study revealed – most Boomers think they will live to age 85, 90 and beyond. Gerontologist Ken Dychtwald has said that Boomers are the first generation in history to reach age 50, and now 60, and know with confidence that they have a third (or more) left of life. When their parents reached 60, they considered themselves lucky if they made it to 75. Therefore, retiring at age 65 made sense, giving you five years or so to travel and see the world, and another five years to play with the grandkids before that "last call."

But Boomers at 50 have a different vision of their own futures. If they have 35, 40 or even more years left, why stop working at age 65 and hang around the sidelines for another several decades? Why marginalize yourself from mainstream society by moving to some sunny climate, where you can join Jerry Seinfeld's parents at the Del Boca Vista condo committee and think that's your big contribution?

We can say with confidence that today's Boomers will do everything they can to avoid the long, slow downhill ride towards a physically or mentally debilitating disease. Instead, they plan on staying vital and participating in life and society until, they hope, the last two weeks of life at 95 when a cold signals a pending visit from the Grim Reaper. At that point, they can say goodbye to their remaining friends and family and die in their sleep at home. Of course, there are some things Boomers cannot ultimately control.

To get a sense of the "vital" mind-set of Boomers, we ask seminar and workshop audiences for a show of hands in agreement with the statement, "My best years are behind me." It's rare that we ever see a single hand go up. No one, at any age, wants to believe that.

So *Viva the Vital!* will become the mantra of Boomers for the next 40 years...and beyond.

Carpenter :: Rosanne Cash :: David Cassidy :: Shaun Cassidy :: Nick Cave :: Cher :: Adam Clayton :: Natalie

Five Vitality Areas

We've identified five areas where Boomers will focus their quest for vitality:

- *Financial Vitality* – This is good news for anyone in the financial services and related fields. Boomers will work to manage their money and maintain their assets, along with "helping" their children and grandchildren with college loans and homes.

- *Physical Vitality* – This relates to both appearance and health and fitness. Boomers already spend countless billions trying to maintain vitality in these areas, and it will only increase in the coming years.

- *Mental Vitality* – The impact of mental diseases like Alzheimer's have made a tremendous impact on today's Boomers, who have seen it in parents, grandparents, and loved ones. They will spend money, time, and energy to avoid a similar fate. Already marketers like Nintendo are capitalizing on this quest for mental strengthening exercises with the 2006 launch of *Brain Age*, a series of games and puzzles for their DDS handheld device. Other companies, like Posit Science of Silicon Valley, are developing a series of computer-based brain exercises to help users increase their mental processing ability. And "neurobotics," consists of exercises anyone can do to strengthen how the brain works. It includes things like brushing your teeth with your opposite hand, or taking a new route to work one day a week.

- *Social Vitality* – As a generation that created and managed social networks in the real world for the last 40-50 years, Boomers will want to maintain their vast social networks. They've invested too much of their lives in it, and are not about to uproot themselves and relocate to some distant retirement community. That's the biggest reason Boomers will likely stay in their communities with their families, rather than joining other "seniors" at an Active Adult community. Plus, Boomers will want to cherish, spoil, and otherwise love their grandchildren, in person. Also, studies by the Corporation for National and Community Service reveal that the Boomer generation volunteers at higher

Cole :: Kim Coles :: Phil Collins :: Coolio :: Alice Cooper :: Chris Cornell :: Elvis Costello :: Christopher Cross

rates than any other – and there are millions more Boomers! So volunteer organizations should reap huge support and rewards over the next 20 or more years tapping into what some are calling America's social capital.

- *Spiritual Vitality* – As Boomers get closer to "what's next" after life, they will reach out to religion or other spiritual organizations to get a better sense of the Grand Plan as it relates to them personally. In 2006, Amazon.com reported that the fastest growing category of book sales was in the religious and spiritual category. Perhaps Dan Brown's *The DaVinci Code* started the trend, but we think Boomers are driving it now.

If your company or organization can help Boomers in this 40-year quest for vitality, in any way, you will be successful. This will be the overarching goal of every Boomer until the last one goes.

Generational Perspective

Written in 1997, the seminal work *The Fourth Turning – What the Cycles of History Tell Us about America's Next Rendezvous with Destiny* by Neil Howe and William Strauss, identifies four reoccurring generational archetypes with four repeating cycles in American history.

Their theories suggest a different future for older Boomers, one where growing old becomes an active, positive phase of life. The Boomer generation that changed societal views on sex, marriage, and procreation will do the same when it comes to death and dying.

Howe and Strauss write, "At the onset of old age, Boomers will do what they have done with every earlier step of the aging process: They will resist it for a while, then dabble in it, and ultimately glorify it….Boomers will establish elegant new insignia of advanced age – flaunting, not avoiding, the natural imprints of time." (Remember Katie Couric's comments about age lines being a sign of wisdom, from Chapter 10?)

They also report that as Boomers "experience their own bodies coping

:: Sheryl Crow :: Billy Ray Cyrus :: Dave Davies :: John Deacon :: Sheila E. :: Sheena Easton :: Enya :: Gloria naturally with decline and death, they will expect government to do the same." The current healthcare system in America is geared, and compensated, to do anything and everything to keep the patient alive. Boomers, at the very end of life, are going to be in a position to return America to a more traditional, and global, view of death and dying. It is a part of life not to be fought against, but honored and accepted. After a certain point, the quality of life deteriorates so much that death becomes a welcome progression.

What will propel this change by the driven, transformational, and "self" centered generation of Boomers?

The answer is simple: Grandchildren.

The Power of Intergenerational Connections

Predicting how today's Boomer Consumers will behave in the future is an inexact science. And the least reliable source for any predictions are, in most cases, Boomers themselves. They can't tell you or anyone else how they might act 10, 15, or 20 years from now. There are too many factors outside of their control, for one. But as Gordon Walker, the one-time hippie and CEO of JABA (Jefferson Area Board on Aging), believes, there is a "Perfect Storm" brewing that suggests to us a clear vision of how Boomers will act in the future.

Walker sees a confluence of events in the coming years:

- Boomers begin reaching their last act, traditionally a time when people look for ways to give back to society, leaving a positive legacy.

- Like "cramming for finals," Boomers will become more spiritual.

- Boomers are in line to derive great personal benefits from the advances in medicine, technology, and healthcare. They could live extraordinarily long and healthy lives.

- Current programs like Social Security, Medicaid, and Medicare are no longer fiscally viable. They lack the financial resources to pay out the obligations due to Boomers. Unless altered soon, these programs won't likely survive the next ten years in their current states and will be forced to make drastic changes.

- Boomers will promote innovation in "age-friendly" housing, land-use, and transportation, thereby demonstrating what is good for older consumers is good for all ages.

One key outcome of these events will likely be the return to intergenerational neighborhoods and households. Until modern times, before the longevity revolution and the creation in the late 1950s of the retirement community, Grandma and Grandpa lived with their children and grandchildren. All generations experienced the effects of aging in front of their very eyes, rather than offstage in an "active adult" community, continuing care retirement community, or nursing home.

Experiencing what Mustafa in "The Lion King" tells young Simba is the "circle of life" will affect adult children and grandchildren in the home. Death and dying is a normal phase, something to be respected and accepted, not denied and fought with every dime.

With the funds for independent living no longer readily available for every future older Boomer, we think they will return to live with their children and grandchildren. This natural, or perhaps necessary, reunification of the generations will have a profound impact on American culture and society, one household at a time. Older Boomers, wondering about their own personal legacies, will be living with their most important legacies – their grandchildren. They will not want to milk systems like Social Security, Medicare, and Medicaid to the detriment of succeeding generations.

Christopher Buckley's book, *Boomsday*, suggests an all-out age war on the horizon unless Boomers elect to kill themselves at age 75 (it is a satire, of course). But Buckley isn't that far off base in that Boomers will do "the right thing" short of suicide. It will be partly out of necessity (the money won't be there), but mostly out of love (not guilt) and the desire to leave a positive legacy for future generations.

Boomers will change death and dying for the good, just as they have changed American society over their first 50 years.

:: Peter Frampton :: Ace Frehley :: Glenn Frey :: Kenny G :: Peter Gabriel :: Crystal Gayle :: Gloria Gaynor ::

BoomBox

The Broken System

Our current healthcare system is geared, and compensated, to do anything and everything to keep the patient alive. We view death as the enemy to be fought tooth and nail, to the last dime. Consequently, our medical care system is becoming slowly crippled by the view that one of our inalienable rights is to fight death with all guns blazing until the very last breath. The Medicaid math speaks for itself.

Medicaid makes up almost 3% of our gross national product already. No issue here. We should spend this much providing basic healthcare for or citizens who are 65+. The issue, or rather crippling statistic, is that an estimated 30% of all Medicaid dollars are spent on the last year of life. That deserves repeating. A third of all Medicaid payments are expended during the last year of life.

If a 77-year-old with any number of aliments, including a slow but nevertheless terminal illness like colon cancer, develops kidney disease they can, and most often do, start an ongoing regimen of dialysis. Costs simply skyrocket. Given our litigious society, doctors strictly follow protocol, making every service, test, and treatment available to keep us alive as long as it is technically feasible. Guilt-ridden adult children who arrive on the medical scene encourage their parents to embrace another treatment. Even when there's a living will involved with "do not resuscitate orders" posted above their hospital beds, families will often "opt out" and push doctors to pursue one more Hail Mary test-treatment scenario. The result — a few more days, weeks, months, maybe even a year added to a person's life. But does it deliver an acceptable quality of life?

Bob Geldof :: Boy George :: Barry Gibb :: Robin Gibb :: Billy Gibbons :: Vince Gill :: David Gilmour :: Anthony

We're not here to judge, but to illustrate the scope of the problem. We're simply pushing the system too far to maintain "life." We think Boomers will change death and dying in America as a result.

Interestingly, our friends across the pond have started to take a different perspective. Great Britain's healthcare system has started to ration healthcare to seniors. If you reach a certain age and develop kidney disease, you can no longer look to Parliament to fund your treatment. Scarce resources must be shared with all generations. The dollars that go into adding months on to a 77-year-old's life now go into better healthcare, better nutrition, better education, for future generations.

We see such a day coming to America, thanks to Boomers getting older.

Intergenerational Solutions, One Step at a Time

One area that's sowing the seeds of change is in Charlottesville, Virginia. Home of the bucolic University of Virginia and rated as one the best places to live in America by *Money* magazine, and *Cities Ranked and Rated*, among others, it is also the location of JABA – the Jefferson Area Board on Aging, an Area Agency on Aging (AAAs) that focuses on this and future generations of older citizens.

Like the rest of the country, the over-65 population of Charlottesville is projected to double by the year 2030. In 2001, JABA and other organizations that serve local seniors came together to formulate a community-wide strategy which they called the 2020 Plan. The plan consisted of what Charlottesville should do now and over the next 20 years to ensure the community could meet the needs of its aging citizens, all the while tapping into what seniors could offer the community. Barely one fourth of the way into implementation, the 2020 Plan is already paying dividends. Walker believes, and we think rightfully so, that making Charlottesville better for older residents makes it better for everyone.

Glise :: Lesley Gore :: Amy Grant :: Al Green :: Arlo Guthrie :: Sammy Hagar :: M.C. Hammer :: Mark Harmon

In Chapter 14 we talked about "Good Grips" now being found in everyone's kitchens, whether they have arthritis or not. Whether for products or communities, good designs that benefit older consumers also help *all* consumers.

For example, JABA is headquartered on Hydraulic Road in Charlottesville. JABA has an adult daycare center and Montessori School within the building. A block or two away on both sides of the road are senior housing facilities. The residents like to come over to the senior center at JABA, but were unable to reach it due to lack of sidewalks and crossing areas. JABA convinced the city and the state Department of Transportation to widen Hydraulic Road, adding walkways and crosswalks.

The focus and reason for the changes were the older citizens. But once the improvements were made, a childcare facility, a park with a playground, and some adjacent neighborhoods also became accessible. Those seniors who could now cross the street started volunteering at the daycare. Those kids at the daycare started crossing the street and visited the senior center, park, and senior housing. Intergenerational interaction took place. Everyone benefited.

Charlottesville was one of, if not the first, region in the country to develop a proposal on how to prepare for the coming age wave. And it has one simple foundation: Create programs, opportunities, facilities, and tools to help foster intergenerational interaction. Get older citizens engaged with younger generations and vice versa. This is the key to and a big solution in selling and marketing to older Boomers.

The Boomer Project's partner, SIR Research, fielded a study in Charlottesville to gauge interest among all generations about the needs and issues facing older citizens. The findings highlight the fact that "aging is everybody's business."

In the study, only half of all residents under age 65 said they personally feel prepared to navigate the challenges of growing older. That anxiety, we think, is the underlying reason why 75% of the respondents said they believe it's important to continue the planning efforts behind the region's 20/20 Plan to make the region a national model in serving its aging population.

If Charlottesville is any indication, Boomers will indeed change what it means to grow old in America – not just on a personal, but on a community and societal level. This may only be a first spark, but it signals a recognition that being able to help and accommodate an older citizenry is important now and will be even more so in the future.

Although no one knows how this intergenerational story will end, it's encouraging to see such a strong beginning.

What Next?

The final act of America's largest, wealthiest, and most influential group is only beginning. There will probably be another twenty years of the "Middle Age of Aquarius" before it reaches "Old Age."

We plan to take stock along the way. As said previously, our best advice for marketers and advertisers is to keep close watch, especially among Boomers who already are your customers, clients, contributors, and constituents. Paying attention to them as they grow older and enter that last season of life is the best and most accurate way of knowing where they may be headed.

And if you are succeeding, please stop by boomerconsumer.com and tell us how it is going. If you need help, let us know that too.

Fasten your seatbelts: It's been a "long, strange trip" so far, and the rest looks to be a fascinating, and bumpy, ride.

:: Whitney Houston :: Janis Ian :: Ice-T :: Billy Idol :: Amy Irving :: Chris Isaak :: Alan Jackson :: Jermaine

Index

Jackson :: LaToya Jackson :: Michael Jackson :: Joan Jett :: Billy Joel :: Elton John :: Howard Jones :: John

Paul Jones :: Jon Bon Jovi :: Naomi Judd :: Wynonna Judd :: Toby Keith :: Chaka Khan :: Lenny Kravitz ::

Huey Lewis :: Kenny Loggins :: Courtney Love :: Lyle Lovett :: Yo-Yo Ma :: Madonna :: Melissa Manchester

McDonald :: Reba McEntire :: Bobby McFerrin :: Meat Loaf :: John Cougar Mellencamp :: Alan Menken ::

George Michael :: Paul Miles :: Mike Mills :: Morrissey :: Olivia Newton-John :: Stevie Nicks :: Peter Noone

:: Ted Nugent :: Ozzy Osbourne :: Donny Osmond :: Marie Osmond :: Shuggie Otis :: Robert Palmer :: Dolly

Parton :: Adrian Paul :: Joe Perry :: Steve Perry :: Neal Pert :: Tom Petty :: Robert Plant :: Iggy Pop :: Prince

:: Bonnie Raitt :: Lionel Richie :: Linda Ronstadt :: Axl Rose :: David Lee Roth :: RuPaul :: Sade :: Carlos

You've read the book, now talk to the authors and get the kind of help your company or organization needs to better connect with today's Boomer Consumer.

The Boomer Project (www.boomerproject.com), an initiative begun in 2003 by Matt Thornhill and by SIR Research (www.sirresearch.com), conducts its own national consumer research to learn how Boomers respond to marketing and advertising messages. We prepare and sell research reports based on those findings (see the Web site for more information). We conduct training seminars and workshops for companies and organizations. We speak at industry, trade and company events and conferences. And we provide customized marketing research and consulting services to organizations ready to take the next step in understanding older Boomers.

Contact Matt Thornhill at matt@boomerproject.com or John Martin at jwm@sirresearch.com for more information.

We're ready to help.

Bruce Springsteen :: Paul Stanley :: Cat Stevens :: Sting :: Michael Stipe :: George Strait :: Donna Summer